Studies in the Modern

GENERAL EDITOR:
Professor of Russian, Uni

1

VERBS OF MOTION

I. P. FOOTE
*Fellow of The Queen's College and
Lecturer in Russian, University of Oxford*

2

THE USE OF THE GENITIVE IN NEGATIVE CONSTRUCTIONS

R. M. DAVISON
Lecturer in Russian, University of Liverpool

CAMBRIDGE
AT THE UNIVERSITY PRESS
1967

CAMBRIDGE UNIVERSITY PRESS
Cambridge, New York, Melbourne, Madrid, Cape Town, Singapore, São Paulo, Delhi

Cambridge University Press
The Edinburgh Building, Cambridge CB2 8RU, UK

Published in the United States of America by Cambridge University Press, New York

www.cambridge.org
Information on this title: www.cambridge.org/9780521113991

© Cambridge University Press 1967

This publication is in copyright. Subject to statutory exception and to the provisions of relevant collective licensing agreements, no reproduction of any part may take place without the written permission of Cambridge University Press.

First published 1967
This digitally printed version 2009

A catalogue record for this publication is available from the British Library

Library of Congress Catalogue Card Number: 67–10255

ISBN 978-0-521-05017-3 hardback
ISBN 978-0-521-11399-1 paperback

CONTENTS

Verbs of motion, *by* I. P. FOOTE — page 4

Text — 4

Bibliography — 33

The use of the genitive in negative constructions, *by* R. M. DAVISON — 34

1 Introduction — 34
2 W. A. Morison's theory — 35
3 Modifications of Morison's theory — 42
   A ви́деть, говори́ть, замеча́ть, понима́ть, знать — 42
   B э́того — 44
   C Parts of the body (Reflexive) — 45
   D Unstressed zero quantity — 46
   E боя́ться, хоте́ть, жела́ть, etc. — 48
   F Equal logical stress of negation — 49
   G Inexplicable uses — 51

4 Minor aspects of the problem — 54
   A Inversion — 54
   B Verbs with the prefix недо- — 56
   C не directly associated with the object — 56

5 The formulation of rules — 57
6 Summary of indications for case choice — 60

Bibliography — 63

VERBS OF MOTION

by I. P. FOOTE

In Russian certain verbs, normally referred to as the 'verbs of motion', have two separate imperfective forms, which, while stating equally the kind of movement involved (going on foot, carrying by conveyance, flying, crawling, etc.), give different information about the nature of the action as it is performed in given circumstances. The group consists of the 'non-descriptive' verbs of motion which indicate, without comment, the basic types of action involving locomotion: going, carrying, flying, crawling, swimming, leading, dragging, etc. Verbs such as мчаться (to rush), шагать (to stride), etc. are not 'basic' verbs of motion and do not come into this category: they have only one imperfective form.

The two imperfectives are normally referred to as the 'determinate' and 'indeterminate'. In the following list the determinate is given first:

бежать	бегать	to run
брести	бродить	to wander (see pp. 5–6, below)
везти	возить	to convey
вести	водить	to lead
гнать	гонять	to drive
ехать	ездить	to ride
идти	ходить	to go on foot
катить	катать	to roll
лезть	лазить	to climb
лететь	летать	to fly
нести	носить	to carry
плыть	плавать	to swim, sail
ползти	ползать	to crawl
тащить	таскать	to drag

Reflexive forms of the transitive verbs in the above list also maintain the determinate/indeterminate distinction, e.g. гнаться/гоняться (to pursue), кататься/катáться (to roll: intransitive), нестись/носиться (to rush), etc.

Between the determinate and the indeterminate verbs in each of the above pairs there is a common distinction, which will be discussed at length below. Not all uses of an individual member of one of these pairs are necessarily paralleled by a use of its partner in a similar sense. Commonly quoted are examples such as таскáться по кабакáм 'to knock about in pubs', unparalleled by тащи́ться in this sense; кати́ть 'to speed along', a meaning not shared by катáть, which itself is used alone in the sense 'to give a ride to someone' (on a boat, bicycle, etc.). The 'special' use of these verbs in these cases results, of course, from the limited nature of the contexts, in which only a particular verb, determinate or indeterminate, is appropriate (Ward: 251-2). Such limited 'non-pair' uses are found especially in figurative or idiomatic expressions, where one member of the pair is used because its implications are valid in the particular context, while those of the other are not (see pp. 32-3, below).

However, though individual verbs may have non-pair uses, there is for each pair a basic sense shared by both determinate and indeterminate members. An exception to this is брести́/броди́ть, in which the semantic relationship is confused: брести́ normally means 'to walk along slowly, with difficulty', броди́ть 'to wander aimlessly'. Isachenko, who excludes this pair from his list of verbs of motion, points out that the relationship between брести́ and броди́ть is not the same as for other determinate/indeterminate pairs: one can say идти́ в гóрод (to go, be on the way to town) and ходи́ть в гóрод (to go on a number of occasions, or there and back), but whereas брести́ в гóрод is possible, броди́ть в гóрод is not. Because of this they do not form a true pair (Isachenko: 12).

The breakdown of the semantic relationship between брести́ and броди́ть is perhaps not surprising: originally брести́ and броди́ть shared the common meaning of 'to ford' (cf. брод, 'a ford'), and the idea implied in the original sense (of slow, impeded or hesitant motion) can still be traced in the modern senses of брести́ and броди́ть. If the relationship between them lacks the clear distinctions that exist between, say, идти́ and ходи́ть, it is simply because there have been rare opportunities for the distinctions to be made, the contextual range of verbs expressing slow, difficult motion being necessarily smaller than that of verbs for 'riding', 'walking', 'carrying'. This does not alter the fact that they are now incomplete in their functions as a determinate/indeterminate pair; nevertheless, it seems reasonable to maintain them in the list of these verbs, since the uses of брести́, such as they are, are determined by the rules for using determinate verbs, and of броди́ть by the rules for using indeterminate verbs.

The difference between determinate and indeterminate verbs has been stated many times in Russian grammars. Most definitions agree in mentioning certain factors as the distinguishing marks of the two types of verbs. The determinate verbs, for example, are described as referring to 'actions taking place in one direction, continuously, at a given moment' (Vinogradov: 1, 460), 'definite, concrete, uninterrupted and directed (*zielgerichtete*) actions' (Ruzicka: 50), 'motion in a definite direction, actually taking place at a given time' (Stilman: 3), 'action in progress at a given point of time' (Birkett: 196), motion taking place in a 'precise direction with an underlying sense of purpose' (Borras and Christian: 163), 'motion tending towards a goal, real or imaginary' (Unbegaun: 222), 'actions in process of occurring and processes which are straightforward in the sense that they are thought of as occurring in only one direction' (Hingley and Binyon: 165). The range of meanings attributed to the 'идти́' type of verbs is also reflected in the number of terms used to describe the category generally: 'actual', 'concrete', 'definite', 'determinate', 'durative', 'non-frequentative' (некратный), 'specific'. The 'ходи́ть' type of verbs are characterized as being the opposite of the 'идти́' verbs in these respects ('actions *not* in one direction, at no special time, etc.'), special mention being made of their use to describe habitual and repeated actions and the capacity for movement (to walk, swim, fly, etc.). This category is described as 'abstract', 'frequentative' (кратный), 'generalized', 'indefinite', 'indeterminate', 'iterative', 'potential'.

A disadvantage of most of these terms is that they refer to only one particular function (or lack of function) of the verbs under discussion. Of those mentioned, the most widely accepted and the most satisfactory, because the broadest in their implications, is the pair 'determinate' and 'indeterminate'.

The general tendency of grammarians to begin by a positive definition of the functions of the determinate verbs and to proceed from that to a largely negative definition of the functions of the indeterminates is reasonable enough. Among the various ways in which movement can be observed and described, the determinate verbs refer to one alone; all others are expressed by the indeterminates, whose functions, therefore, are varied and numerous, united only by their inapplicability to 'determinate' action.

Determinate verbs are used to describe a simple movement along a line (линейное движение). This is what is meant by 'in one direction' in the definitions quoted above. Diagrammatically, such movement would be represented by a plain arrow: ⟶ (not necessarily straight). 'Direction', as such, may be unimportant or irrelevant, and perhaps the use of the word in definitions of determinate verbs introduces rather too precise a flavour into what may be quite a casual action (this is especially true of definitions which talk of 'definite' or 'precise' direction—'definable' would be generally better).

An essential quality of the determinate verbs is that they refer to *progressive* motion, motion that involves the subject (or object in the case of the transitive verbs) in a *change of location*. The person or thing moving or moved may have no special interest in where the movement will lead. Although, more often than not, the action of a determinate verb is motivated by an intention of getting oneself or something somewhere, this is not essential, and, providing the action remains simple (i.e. advancing along a line), it can be quite aimless, or even unconscious. Direction in the normal sense is irrelevant in cases such as Приятно идти под дождём (It's nice to walk in the rain), where all the subject is interested in is the pleasure derived from indulging in an action under certain conditions; or Поезд идёт быстро (The train is going fast), where what matters is the rate of progress. Another disadvantage of the phrase 'in one direction' is that it might be mistakenly thought to imply movement in a straight line. A person may walk in zigzags, but can still progress in a general line that takes him away from some notional starting point towards some notional goal (e.g. Он зигзагами шёл к дому, 'He zigzagged towards the house').

Another feature of motion as expressed by determinate verbs is 'actuality': the action is envisaged as 'actual' or in progress (cf. the definitions above). This does not always or necessarily mean a *particular* or *concrete* performance of the action, since, as we shall see below, determinate verbs can be used to refer to habitual or typical actions (e.g. Каждый день в 9 он идёт в контору, 'Every day at 9 he goes to the office'), as well as to potential actions (e.g. in general statements like Приятно идти под дождём above), but most often they will be found referring to specific movements.

The idea of actuality conveyed by the determinate verbs accounts for their use to refer to actions due to take place in the future (e.g. Лётом отéц везёт семью́ в СССР, 'In the summer Father is taking (= will take) the family to the USSR', etc.). Though other verbs are occasionally used in a similar way (Сего́дня ве́чером я игра́ю в ша́хматы, 'I am playing chess this evening'; О́сенью он поступа́ет в университе́т, 'He is going to university in the autumn'), none enjoys the full flexibility to act in this way possessed by the determinate verbs of motion. The context is always the same: the action referred to is one already arranged or decided on, and so is as good as taking place. To be expressed by идти́, etc., such actions must always be straightforward actions of going, etc., 'determinate' in the sense already mentioned. (The present tense of indeterminate verbs cannot be used to refer to future action.)[1]

Actuality is, though, not an exclusive attribute of determinate verbs. The distinction commonly made between indeterminate verbs such as ходи́ть as 'general' or 'abstract' and their determinate counterparts as 'specific' or 'concrete' is a fair one in certain usages (Он хо́дит в шко́лу, 'He goes to school', a general statement, with no reference to any specific occasion of going, but Он идёт в шко́лу, 'He is going to school', a statement that the subject is now on a given occasion on his way to school). But motion on a specific occasion can also be expressed by ходи́ть: Он сейча́с хо́дит по ко́мнате (At the moment he is walking about the room) is no less 'actual' or 'concrete' than Он идёт в шко́лу—the action is in progress at the moment of observation. The difference here lies not in the actuality or potentiality of the action, but in the nature of the movement.

If 'determinate' motion is simple progressive motion along a

---

[1] Though one must always be wary of drawing conclusions from the correlation of Russian and English usage, one might usefully compare the Russian use of the present tense of determinate verbs and the English use of the continuous present to express the future in such contexts. Like the determinates, the English continuous present (is going, is carrying, etc.) emphasizes the action as actually in progress, as happening now, so, when it is necessary to express some future action as already in train, we find it used for this purpose (cf. the translations of the examples above).

line, there are two ways in which motion might be 'indeterminate': first, by being motion taking place non-progressively along a number of lines (i.e. in different directions), or along a single line a number of times, or forward and back along a single line (i.e. 'complex' motion of various kinds); and secondly, by being motion envisaged in relation to *no line at all* (i.e. 'non-contextual' motion).

All actions expressed by verbs of motion might, therefore, be placed in three groups in descending order of complexity, according to context:
(1) Complex actions (expressed by the indeterminate).
(2) Simple actions (expressed by the determinate).
(3) Non-contextual actions (expressed by the indeterminate).

Any complex ('ходи́ть' type) action described by an indeterminate verb must be made up of a number of simple ('идти́' type) actions. Someone who travels regularly to London might say during any single performance of the journey towards London: 'Я е́ду в Ло́ндон.' If, though, he views all the journeys as a collective whole, to describe his regular practice, then he will say: 'Я е́зжу в Ло́ндон.' Conversely, any 'ходи́ть' action can be broken down into its 'идти́' components. As Forsyth points out, Он хо́дит по ко́мнате is a complex action made up of a number of individual actions, and if you look more closely at the mover and pinpoint any particular part of his course, then you move out of the range of the complex into the range of the simple action and switch from the indeterminate to the determinate verb (Forsyth: 149). In the example quoted (Он хо́дит по ко́мнате), if the focus of attention is narrowed, one can say: 'Вот он идёт от две́ри к окну́, тепе́рь идёт от окна́ к ками́ну', etc. It is simply a matter of how the action is viewed. If it is viewed from a distance, as it were, in the mass, or over a period of time, the observer has only the impression of a collective action (indeterminate); if it is viewed more closely, at a particular moment, the perspective of the observer will be limited to only one stage or 'leg' of the action (determinate); then, if the observer narrows his view still further, so that he sees only the subject, detached from his surroundings, performing movements unrelated to any *line of action*, he will again be in the sphere of the indeterminate. An analogy might be drawn with forest (collective), tree (singulative) and timber (the physical content of both).

It could be said that an indeterminate verb, except when used to refer to 'non-contextual' actions, *says more* than a determinate. It always introduces some view of motion that goes beyond the plain fact of a person moving forward along a line. In an important respect the determinate can be claimed as the more basic verb, since it is the determinate that refers to movement in its essential moment: movement as opposed to a state of rest. People in a train would say at the moment it begins to move from the station: 'Éдем'; others on the platform would say of the train: 'Идёт.' It is the simple fact of movement that is expressed here, and éздить, ходи́ть would be unthinkable, since they express notions of greater complexity or abstraction.

This fundamental aspect of the determinate verbs is seen also in the use of the perfectives пойти́, etc., in the sense of 'set off', 'get moving', etc.

In certain respects the determinate and indeterminate verbs represent a kind of aspect system, and some grammarians refer to these verbal categories as 'sub-aspects' (подвиды). The analogy with aspects is justifiable at least in the respect that different verbs are used for what is generically the same action (flying is flying, whether expressed by лете́ть or лета́ть), depending on how it is viewed. Because they are used only within particular limited contexts the determinate verbs might be described as a kind of 'restricted' imperfective (the indeterminates being 'unrestricted'). Certain comparisons may be drawn in this connection between determinate verbs and verbs of perfective aspect. Both refer to actions of *one* particular kind (determinate action, perfective action), while their pair verb (the indeterminate, the imperfective) is a general-purpose verb, used to describe the action in all its other manifestations. As a result of their similarity as verbs of restricted action determinate verbs and perfective verbs tend to be used in similar kinds of situations. This is so in the case of negative statements and commands. In negative statements the determinate is used primarily when the specific non-performance of an action expected or intended is envisaged, e.g. Прика́зано бы́ло атакова́ть ба́ки...А лю́ди в ата́ку не шли (Nekrasov, В око́пах Сталингра́да), 'Orders were given to attack the cisterns, but the men didn't attack'—they were expected to, but didn't (compare the use of the indeterminate for straightforward negation: Он сего́дня на рабо́ту не ходи́л, 'He didn't go to work today'). This is

the kind of situation when a perfective will be used with a negative
—e.g. Он нé дал женé дéнег, 'He didn't give his wife the money'
(on a particular occasion and when he might have been expected
to); cf. the sentence Он не давáл женé дéнег, which could also
refer to a particular occasion, but without any special point being
made of the fact that he did not give his wife the money. In negative commands, too, the determinate verbs are used in the same
kinds of situations as perfectives. They express an urgent injunction against a particular performance of the action, e.g. in warnings against an action felt to be imminent:

| Не идите по льду! | Don't walk on the ice. |
| Не несите ребёнка дáльше! Там опáсно. | Don't take the child any further—it's dangerous.[1] |

These may be compared with examples of the perfective imperative in negative commands with the same import, such as

| Смотри, не упади в рекý! | Mind you don't fall in the river![2] (The implication is that you are in some danger of doing so.) |

Though these comparisons may be helpful in understanding the
nature of the determinate verbs, it must, of course, be borne firmly
in mind that the determinate verbs are always and only imperfective in aspect.

Although perfectives may be formed from both determinate and
indeterminate verbs, there is in the perfective aspect no system of
determinate/indeterminate pairs. The relationship between пойти
and походить, for example, is not the same as that between идти
and ходить—пойти means 'to get moving', 'to embark on or
complete a single action of going' (to some goal); походить means
'to do a bit of walking'.

However, although the system of paired verbs is not maintained
in the perfective, one still finds the basic notions of the determinate
(simple 'line' movement) and of the indeterminate (complex or
non-contextual movement) preserved in the perfectives formed
from them. Thus, for example, повести, погнáть, пойти, потащить have meanings of starting to lead, drive, go, drag, of setting
out on or accomplishing a specific, non-complex action of the type
expressed by the verb. On the other hand, perfectives such as

---

[1] Examples quoted by Mazon (85).
[2] Also in Mazon (98).

11

забегать, пролетать, объездить, formed from indeterminate verbs, refer to the same kinds of actions as those expressed by indeterminate imperfectives. Intransitive verbs of motion usually give rise to two types of perfective based on the indeterminate: (*a*) intransitive—e.g. заходить, 'start walking (about)', полетать, 'do a bit of flying, fly around for a time', съездить, 'drive/ride somewhere and come back'; and (*b*) transitive—e.g. выездить, 'break in' (a horse), пробегать (километр, час), 'run (a kilometre, for the space of an hour)'.[1] The intransitive perfectives, it can be seen, retain the 'indeterminate' idea of complex or undirected action; заходить, for instance, indicates the onset of walking, without envisaging any direction or goal; полетать suggests a period of flying without any idea of getting anywhere; similarly, perfectives of the reflexive type набегаться (to have had enough of running), наползаться (to have had enough of crawling), emphasize the physical effort of running, crawling, without reference to any line along which the action is carried out. Equally, the transitive perfectives formed from intransitive indeterminates—such as облетать (imperfective облётывать), 'to test', 'run in' (an aircraft), выездить (imperfective выезжать), 'to break in' (a horse), изъездить (imperfective изъезживать), 'to drive/ride round and visit a lot or all of...'—all indicate the results of a complex series of actions which could not possibly be represented as involving any simple 'line' movement.

Characteristic of perfectives formed from the indeterminate of transitive verbs is that they convey the sense of shifting, carrying, etc., as a complex process involving a number of journeys, e.g. перевозить (to transfer by conveying in a number of journeys), наносить (to bring (a quantity of something) in a number of journeys).

---

[1] Perfectives such as these formed from indeterminate verbs by prefixation are, in the case of some verbs (водить, возить, гонять, летать, носить, ходить), homonyms of compound imperfectives formed in the same way, e.g. the perfective заходить has the same form as заходить, imperfective of зайти. Homonymy is avoided in the case of бродить, ездить, лазить, плавать, since the compound imperfectives are formed in -бредать, -езжать, -лезать, -плывать; in the case of катать and таскать, since the compound imperfectives are in -катывать, -таскивать; in the case of бегать and ползать, since there is differentiation by stress—the perfectives keep the stress on the same syllable as the indeterminate (забегать, заползать, etc.), the imperfectives have the stress on the final syllable (забегать, заползать, etc.).

The following section is intended to demonstrate the range of uses of the determinate and indeterminate verbs. Since the ideas expressed by the former are fewer than those expressed by the latter, it will be convenient to start with the determinate group. If in the examples some verbs appear to be over-represented (идти́, е́хать, нести́, etc.), while others occur infrequently or not at all (e.g. кати́ть, гнать, лезть), this is simply because of their relative frequency in use; the points made about examples with идти́, etc., can be taken as valid for any verb of this group.

DETERMINATE VERBS

The idea of simple 'line' motion is basic whenever an action is seen as in process and directed towards a stated goal, as in:

Куда́ идёте?	Where are you going?
Идём в кино́.	We're going to the cinema.
Он несёт посы́лку на по́чту.	He's taking a parcel to the post-office.

Direction need not be stated, or even implied. The emphasis then is placed on the plain fact of movement in a given context.

По́езд шёл бы́стро.	The train was going fast.
Самолёт...горе́л, но продолжа́л лете́ть.	The plane was on fire, but still went on flying.
(Chukovsky, Балти́йское не́бо)	

In these two examples, although no direction is mentioned, the actions envisaged are clearly straightforward movements that advance the subjects along a line.

The action may have the appearance of complexity, but, providing it advances the subject (or object) along a general line of movement, the determinate verb must be used:

Она́ шла с ле́стницы на ле́стницу, из этажа́ в эта́ж.	She went from staircase to staircase, from floor to floor.
(Chukovsky, *op. cit.*)	

The person in question is following a deliberate course. Ходи́ла in the same sentence would suggest random wandering from one part of the building to another without any plan or progress—it would suitably describe, for instance, the movements of someone lost in the building. (Equally well, of course, it could refer to a repeated action.)

The idea of *progress* is implicit in the following use of determinate infinitives:

Шинéль...скúнул, чтоб лéгче бежáть бы́ло. (Nekrasov, В окóпах Сталингрáда)	He threw off his greatcoat to make running easier.
Я...хотéл часть вещéй вы́кинуть, чтоб лéгче бы́ло нестú. (*Ibid.*)	I wanted to throw out some of the things to make it easier to carry.
Тропúнка... сдéлалась такóй скóльзкой, что стáло трýдно идтú. (Chukovsky, Балтúйское нéбо)	The path got so slippery that it became hard to walk.

In each of these sentences the idea of *getting along*, of *making progress* (by running, carrying, walking), can be noted. Compare the following general statements:

...окóпы слúшком ýзки, рáненых трýдно носúть. (Nekrasov, *op. cit.*)	The trenches are too narrow, (which makes it) hard for carrying wounded.
По дорóге идтú лéгче, нéжели без дорóги. (Gogol', Áвторская úсповедь)	It is easier to go along a road than across country.

In the first statement, which might be claimed as more specific in context than the absolute proposition of the second, the progressive idea is lacking. The narrowness of the trenches impedes *any* carrying of wounded; no idea of *getting* the wounded anywhere is present. On the other hand, the second sentence has just this idea of 'getting along' uppermost: you make better progress if you walk along a road than if you walk over broken ground.

The determinate, expressing progressive motion, is the natural choice in contexts where any figurative 'advancing' or 'marching forward' is involved, as in всё идёт к лýчшему (everything is for the best), идтú в нóгу с жúзнью (to keep pace with life), or in the example:

Клянёмся тебé, товáрищ Стáлин, ...всегдá идтú в пéрвой шерéнге. (Nikolayeva, Бúтва в путú)	Comrade Stalin, we pledge ourselves always to march in the front rank! (understood 'in the march of progress').

Determinate verbs are regularly used with reference to the line followed by inanimate objects (roads, fences, wires, etc.), since, again, the course followed is necessarily a straightforward one along a given line, e.g.

Чéрез фóрточку с ýлицы шли проводá к двум полевы́м телефóнам. (Ostrovsky, Как закалúлась сталь)	From the street ran wires through the ventilating-pane to two field-telephones.

Кругóм лес, зигзáгом бежи́т вниз подъéздная дорóга. (*Ibid.*)	There's forest all round; the approach road runs zigzagging down below.
Жи́рная крáсная ли́ния ползёт чéрез всю кáрту. (Nekrasov, *op. cit.*)	A thick red line crawls right across the map.

Идти́, etc., are also used of what might be termed 'steady stream' actions, in which there is a constant movement of objects, material, etc., proceeding always in the same direction, e.g.

Маши́ны иду́т — однá за другóй, однá за другóй. (Nekrasov, *op. cit.*)	Cars go along, one after the other, one after the other.
Штóрмы шли за штóрмами. (Chukovsky, *op. cit.*)	There were gales, one after the other.

This use of идти́ underlies its use in phrases such as дождь идёт, снег идёт, in which the constant, one-way movement of the rain and snow is envisaged. The same is true of expressions referring to the passage of time (гóды шли; врéмя бежи́т; врéмя лети́т); and it is found again in phrases which describe the issuing of smoke, the emanation of smells, the flowing of blood, etc. (дым идёт из трубы́, 'smoke comes out of the chimney'; от негó несёт табакóм, 'he smells of tobacco'; кровь идёт, 'blood is flowing').

Determinate verbs are used in general statements of fact, whenever simple one-way motion is envisaged.

Отсюда до стáнции 5 киломéтров, идти́ пешкóм далекó.	The station is 5 kilometres from here —it's (too) far to walk.
Ехать до негó на маши́не нáдо бы́ло мину́т 10. (Maysky, Дни испытáний)	It took about 10 minutes to get to his place by car.

In contexts such as these, where the distance or time involved in getting to a particular place is mentioned, determinate verbs are regularly used. (If, though, what is envisaged is more complex—going and coming back, for instance—then the indeterminate will be used, even though the context might from the English point of view appear the same, cf.

Óсенью стáло ху́же: нельзя́ бы́ло сидéть на крылéчке, в кинематóграф ходи́ть — далекó. (Panova, Временá гóда)	It was worse in the autumn: they couldn't sit out on the steps, and it was a long trek to the cinema (and back).)

Similarly in sentences indicating the time taken over a simple journey (i.e. not a 'round trip') the determinate is used:

40 киломе́тров до о́зера тащи́лись они́ бо́льше двух часо́в.
(Chukovsky, Балти́йское не́бо)

It took them over two hours to struggle the 40 kilometres to the lake.

Письмо́ шло тогда́ из Петербу́рга в Вя́тку дней 11–15.
(El'sberg, Салтыко́в-Щедри́н)

In those days a letter took some 11–15 days to get from Petersburg to Vyatka.

The idea of simply *going along*, of performing the basic action of the verb, is uppermost in the following example:

Неизъясни́мо хорошо́ плыть по Во́лге осе́нней но́чью. (Gor'ky)

It is indescribably pleasant to sail on the Volga on an autumn night.

This statement might equally well be made with пла́вать substituted for плыть, but it would introduce an unnecessary elaboration ('sailing *about*') to the basic simple movement ('sailing *along*'). Determinate verbs are normal in contexts where the idea of simple 'engaging in the action' is in mind, the action here being reduced to its basic component, e.g.

Го́нчий пёс рожда́ется, что́бы гнать зве́ря-врага́.
(Kazakov, Аркту́р — го́нчий пёс)

A hound is born to chase its enemy, the wild animal.

In definitions of the functions of determinate and indeterminate verbs it is usually stated that indeterminates are used whenever repeated or habitual actions are described, but Russian usage shows that (at least for the English student of Russian) this statement needs qualification, for determinate verbs do often occur in sentences relating to regular or customary actions. What must be borne in mind is that indeterminate verbs refer chiefly to actions seen as *complex* or *collective*, while determinate verbs describe actions viewed as *simple* or *singulative* (not necessarily *single*, i.e. taking place only once). A habitual action can be viewed in one of two ways:

(1) It can be seen 'collectively', as the sum, that is, of all the individual actions taken together. This is especially the case if it is referred to absolutely, detached from any delimiting context, and in such cases the indeterminate verb is used, e.g.

Он ходи́л к ней раз в неде́лю.
(Turgenev, Запи́ски охо́тника)

He went to see her once a week.

Вы ча́сто сюда́ хо́дите...купа́ться?
(Ostrovsky, Как закаля́лась сталь)

Do you often come here to bathe?

(2) It can be seen as a simple action. This 'simple' view will be taken whenever a typical single occasion is referred to as exempli-

fying the general practice (a kind of *pars pro toto*), and in such cases the determinate verb will be used—provided always, of course, that the recurring action exemplified is one of simple 'line' movement and not indeterminate by nature. Although the action takes place recurrently, the thoughts of the speaker concentrate on a typical instance, and he sees the repeated action crystallized in a single manifestation of it ('action réitérée ramenée à l'unité', in Mazon's phrase). In this use the determinate functions in a similar way to the perfective future when it is used to describe habitual actions, e.g.

Дéдушка знáет, когдá какóй из них прихóдит, и всякому йли махнёт рукóй..., йли приотвóрит окнó и кликнет. (Saltykov-Shchedrin, Пошехóнская старинá)	Grandfather knows when any of them comes, and to each he waves or opens the window to call them.

There are two main types of context in which a simple view will be taken of a repeated action. The first might be called 'exemplary' contexts, and the second 'routine' contexts. Though there is no real difference between 'exemplary' and 'routine' uses of the determinates (in both the speaker focuses his view on a single typical instance of the action), it will be convenient to list the examples under these separate headings.

(*a*) *Exemplary*

The following are some examples of the use of the 'exemplary' determinate:

В ней [передовйце] осуждáлись командиры, ведýщие лйчно свой подразделéния в атáку. (Nekrasov, В окóпах Сталингрáда)	It [the leading article] contained a condemnation of commanders who personally lead their units in attack.
Вылезáют и, éсли когó-нибудь убйло, закáпывают тут же на берегý ...Рáненых ведýт в санчáсть. (*Ibid.*)	[When the bombing stops] they come out, and if anybody's been killed they bury them there on the bank. They take the wounded to the dressing-station.
Лю́ди тóже иногдá умирáют. Их кладýт в...гробы́ и несýт по ýлицам. (Panova, Серёжа)	People too die sometimes. They put them in coffins and carry them through the streets.
Пáпа и мáма чáсто расставáлись. Пáпа пéрвым éхал в какóй-нибудь гóрод, . . . потóм . . . приезжáла мáма. (Kochetov, Мóлодость с нáми)	Father and Mother often separated. Father would go first to some town and Mother would come later.

In the first example the reference is to commanders who might *on any occasion* lead their units in attack, and the 'any occasion' is seen as one occasion. The fact that certain commanders do this could be expressed absolutely, but then the indeterminate verb would be required: Некоторые командиры лично водят свои подразделения в атаку. In the remaining examples the limitation of the action to a single context is strongly felt because there is an implied notion of 'time when' ('*When* (on any particular occasion) the bombing stops...', '*When* people die...', etc.), and this encourages the use of the determinate to describe an example of 'what happens when...'. This kind of limitation, implied in the examples given, comes out with greater clarity when the action is expressly pinpointed—for instance by a conditional clause, as in the following examples:

Если солнце начинало слишком припекать, они...бежали на набережную...и...купались.
(Chukovsky, Балтийское небо)

If it got very hot in the sun, they would run down to the embankment and bathe.

Если случались затруднения, [он] бежал ко мне.
(Tendryakov, Чрезвычайное)

If any difficulties arose, he would come running to me.

Or if the verb of motion itself stands in the subordinate clause:

Когда мать шла из дому, он... оглядывал её — всё ли на ней прилично и красиво.
(Panova, Времена года)

Whenever his mother went out, he inspected her to make sure everything about her dress was nice and proper.

The same thing can be seen in relative clauses:

Тут...было самое людное место в городе. Сюда сходились все, кто шёл за водой с Невского, с Гороховой... (Chukovsky, *op. cit.*)

This was the busiest place in the city, for all the people from the Nevsky, the Gorokhovaya, gathered here when they went to fetch water.

Here, шёл is used of anyone who on any occasion went to fetch water (compare командиры, ведущие... (= командиры, которые ведут) in the example quoted above).

(b) Routine

In describing habitual or routine actions there is a natural tendency to 'actualize' or typify the action in question. In the following examples regular or habitual actions are referred to:

Обы́чно Никола́й заходи́л за А́нной Пантелеймо́новной в библиоте́ку, и они́ вме́сте шли домо́й. (Nekrasov, В родно́м го́роде)	As a rule Nikolay called for Anna Panteleymonovna at the library and they would walk home together.
Ва́ся ждал её,...и они́ вдвоём шли гуля́ть. (Chukovsky, *op. cit.*)	Vasya used to wait for her, and the pair of them would go for a walk.

Viewed absolutely, these actions would properly be stated by indeterminate verbs: Никола́й и А́нна Пантелеймо́новна вме́сте ходи́ли домо́й; Они́ с Ва́сей ходи́ли гуля́ть. But шли is used in these examples because the speaker shifts himself from an 'absolute' to a 'contextual' view of the action and sees it as though it were taking place before him.[1] Here, the 'contextual' view of the action is particularly determined by the fact that the actions of 'going home', 'going for a walk', are seen as part of a chain of actions (заходи́л...шли..., ждал...шли...). In such contexts there may be emphasis on the action as a directed action, which takes the subject forward to some new activity, the focus of interest progressing with him along the line he follows. In the example

Лу́нин остава́лся в ПА́РМе до обе́да, пото́м шёл в столо́вую. (Chukovsky, *op. cit.*)	Lunin used to stay in the PARM ['field workshop'] till dinner time and then go to the mess.

there is a shift of interest from the workshop to the mess. What happens in the mess will now be told, or the interest may shift further to some new field. The emphasis is, therefore, on *progressive*, simple movement, and the use of the indeterminate in such a case would introduce, inappropriately, the idea of a complex action. This difference between the use of the determinate and the indeterminate is clear in the following example:

Но Тата́ренко по-пре́жнему ка́ждый ве́чер ходи́л купа́ться на за́падный мыс. По́сле купа́нья он шёл у́жинать в земля́нку во́зле аэродро́ма. (Chukovsky, *op. cit.*)	But Tatarenko still went to the west cape every evening to bathe. After his bathe he would go and have supper in the dugout by the aerodrome.

Here the first sentence is a general statement referring to Tatarenko's habitual journeys to bathe. Contextually free, the

---

[1] Comparison with English usage shows a parallel here. In contexts of this kind, in which past habitual actions are referred to, where Russian uses the determinate, the tendency in English is to use 'would...' ('He used to wait for her and they *would* go...'), which has the same kind of 'actualizing' force as the determinate.

action can be regarded as a collective one and so the indeterminate verb is used. In the second sentence, however, the action envisaged is contextually limited by по́сле купа́нья and what Tatarenko did when he reached the dugout, and this increases the demand for the determinate. Compare the following sentences:

Ка́ждый день она́ с ра́ннего утра́ шла в ба́ню и проводи́ла там всё вре́мя до ве́чера.
(Chukovsky, Балти́йское не́бо)

Every day she would go to the baths first thing and stay there right through to the evening.

До войны́, ко́нчив рабо́ту, он шёл в пивну́ю и там до хрипоты́ спо́рил.
(Erenburg, Бу́ря)

Before the war he'd go to the pub after work and there argue himself hoarse.

In both, the determinate verb is necessary because the speaker is referring to a typical action, and also because the action of going to the baths, to the pub, is followed by a statement of what happened when the subject got there. In both cases и там in the second half of the sentence requires the use of a verb of *simple* motion in the first.

Perhaps the clearest examples of contextual limitation are provided by sentences cataloguing lists of activities, daily routines, etc. The following are some examples:

А у́тром Лежа́н шёл на заво́д..., разгова́ривал с инжене́рами, пото́м отправля́лся в городско́й комите́т. (Erenburg, Девя́тый вал)

In the morning Lejean would go to the factory, chat with the engineers, then go off to the town council.

Ежедне́вно от 9 до полу́дня он принима́л больны́х..., а по́сле полу́дня е́хал...в другу́ю больни́цу.
(Chekhov, Попрыгу́нья)

Every day from 9 till midday he saw patients, and after midday he went to another hospital.

Ежедне́вно, встя́вши...в 11, О́льга Ива́новна игра́ла на роя́ле и́ли же...писа́ла чтó-нибудь ма́сляными кра́сками. Потом, в пе́рвом часу́, она́ е́хала к свое́й портни́хе.
(*Ibid.*)

Every day, after rising at 11, Ol'ga Ivanovna played the piano or did some oil-painting. Then, between 12 and 1, she would go to her dressmaker.

Ра́нними утра́ми...Бакса́нов заки́дывал за́ спину ружьё, станови́лся на лы́жи и...шёл встреча́ть зарю́. (Kochetov, Секрета́рь обко́ма)

In the early morning Baksanov would sling his gun on his back, get on his skis and go to meet the dawn.

Such uses of determinate verbs to describe repeated or habitual actions are, as was already stated, basically no different from the 'exemplary' uses quoted above. Forsyth emphasizes that the speaker limits his perspective to a particular time of day, etc., and so envisages the action as taking place at that moment, directed towards its goal (Forsyth: 149). To this it might be added that in such cases the use of the determinate verb is not a question of stylistic choice (as is the case when the perfective future is used as a stylistic alternative to the imperfective past or present to describe habitual actions), for the speaker has no choice. Given the context of other routine actions, stated or implied, if simple, though repeated, 'line' movement is referred to, the determinate verb must be used.

In some cases, however (not those referred to above), a stylistic choice between determinate and indeterminate verbs can be exercised. Compare

Поездá на э́той доро́ге иду́т ме́дленно.	The trains on this line go slowly.

and

Поездá в Итáлии хо́дят бы́стро.	In Italy the trains travel fast.

or

Трамвáй по э́той ли́нии идёт че́рез кáждые че́тверть часá.	On this route the trams go every quarter of an hour.

and

Трамвáй по э́той ли́нии хо́дит че́рез кáждые че́тверть часá.	On this route the trams go every quarter of an hour.

In both pairs the statements refer to the same (or similar) facts, and there is no reason for the different verbs used other than that the speaker is choosing his perspective of the action. In the examples using determinate verbs the speaker thinks of the speed of the trains or the succession of the trams in a more graphic way; his viewpoint is rather that of the traveller, say, who can speak familiarly of the speed of the trains, or who stands at the tramstop watching the trams approach at regular intervals (вот идёт трамвáй, вот идёт друго́й). The sentences with the indeterminate verbs present the same facts, but less graphically, in a more detached way—from the viewpoint, say, of a traffic administrator or someone making a general statement about transport arrangements.

The following example shows the author switching his viewpoint in mid-sentence in what might seem a rather perverse way:

Маломо́щные колхо́зы вози́ли прода́ва́ть свой проду́кты на база́р в райце́нтр, колхо́зы покре́пче, име́ющие по 4, 5 грузовы́х маши́н, везли́ на база́ры областно́го го́рода. (Tendryakov, Паде́ние Ива́на Чупро́ва)	The small collective farms took their produce for sale to the market in the district centre, but the rather bigger ones with 4 or 5 lorries took (theirs) to the markets in the *oblast'* town.

Here, it seems, the shift from the indeterminate (which would be expected in such contexts) to the determinate is accounted for by the more striking nature of the fact that some farms sent produce to the *oblast'* centre. The more striking fact receives the more graphic statement. The following is another example from the same work:

Тепе́рь у колхо́за «Кра́сная заря́» 5 грузовы́х маши́н, и на них мя́со, ма́сло, муку́ из Пожа́ров везу́т пря́мо в го́род.	The 'Red Dawn' collective farm has now got 5 lorries and in them they take the meat, butter and flour straight from Pozhary into the town.

Here, again, the writer takes a more graphic view of what is a habitual action, and, again, one might point to a cause (or, at least, a contributory cause) for this vivid reporting: here, the striking fact is that produce is now carried 'пря́мо в го́род'.

However perplexing these shifts of perspective may at times appear, there is, at least, one hard and fast rule—that is that the shift in perspective can only take place from indeterminate to determinate, never from determinate to indeterminate. While it is always possible to present graphically to oneself a general, abstract action as individual and concrete, it is never possible to do the reverse.

INDETERMINATE VERBS

Indeterminate verbs refer to actions that lack the contextual limitations characteristic of the determinate verbs. These actions can be grouped under two broad headings:

(1) Actions in course of taking place which are complex, or actions taking place at different times which are viewed collectively.

(2) The action itself, not seen in application to any particular journey or line of movement.

In neither of these types of action, it will be seen, is any kind of *progressive* idea present: none of the above cases is concerned with any *effective change of location* of the subject (or object), which is the essential condition of any action expressed by a determinate verb.

If we examine examples of indeterminates used to describe actions under the first heading, we find three main types of 'complexity'.

(a) In the first place, complexity may be due to the action taking place in various directions, e.g.

Теперь они вместе собирают грибы, ползают по траве… (Aksyonov, Пора, мой друг, пора)	Now they gather mushrooms together, crawling about in the grass.
Вальган ходил из угла в угол в своей комнате. (Nikolayeva, Битва в пути)	Val'gan paced his room from corner to corner.
Экскурсантов возили в автобусе по городу.	The trippers were taken round the town in a bus.

In each of these examples the persons concerned are moving in various directions (alternatively, in no particular direction), and are not seen as progressing along a line of movement which would get them somewhere. The distinction between indeterminate and determinate verbs is of special importance in sentences such as the last one, where по + dative is used to denote the 'area of action'. The trippers in this sentence were simply taken round the town, going from one place of interest to another without any overriding aim of reaching some goal. In the following example with по городу the determinate verb makes it clear that the subject is actually on her way somewhere:

Надо начинать жизнь сначала, думала я, пока шла по городу. (Aksyonov, Апельсины из Марокко)	I've got to start life all over again, I thought to myself as I walked through the town.

The idea of complex direction may result from the observation of a number of subjects moving at the same time in different directions. Each individual movement may be a simple, progressive one, but the collective idea is of complexity, e.g.

Люди ходили по улице.	There were people walking in the street.
Внизу люди бегают, как муравьи. (Nekrasov, В родном городе)	Down below people are running about like ants.

It would be theoretically possible to split any of the above complex actions into its determinate components (Экскурсантов возили по го́роду: сперва́ везли́ по у́лице Го́рького, пото́м везли́ по Кра́сной пло́щади...; Лю́ди ходи́ли по у́лице: рабо́чий шёл на фа́брику, ма́льчик шёл в шко́лу...). It should, though, be noted that multiple action of this kind can also be seen as a number of directed actions, with the determinate being used, e.g.

| На у́лицах лю́ди с тюка́ми, теле́жками. Бегу́т, спотыка́ются. (Nekrasov, В око́пах Сталингра́да) | In the streets there are people with bundles and hand-carts. They run stumblingly... |

Any kind of circular movement, which, by nature, is non-progressive, requires the use of the indeterminate verb:

| Защища́ясь от «Мессершми́ттов», они́ тепе́рь ходи́ли друг за дру́гом по кру́гу. (Chukovsky, Балти́йское не́бо) | They were now circling round after each other, trying to keep off the Messerschmitts. |
| Он вприся́дку ходи́л вокру́г Со́ни. (*Ibid.*) | He danced (went) round Sonya on his haunches. |

Actions of complex direction include also those involving movement to and from a stated point—so-called 'round-trip' actions:

| В про́шлом году́ они́ е́здили во Фра́нцию. | Last year they went to France. |
| Вчера́ мы ходи́ли в кино́. | We went to the cinema yesterday. |

Sometimes the idea of 'fetching' is present:

| Остроса́блин то́лько что лета́л на аэродро́м за горю́чим... (Chukovsky, *op. cit.*) | Ostrosablin had just been back to the aerodrome to get fuel. |

This use of е́здить, ходи́ть, лета́ть, etc.—which is limited to the past tense—is often regarded as an eccentric feature of the indeterminate verbs. In fact, the question is not strictly concerned with indeterminate verbs as such, but rather with the imperfective aspect and its uses in the past tense. In reality, there is nothing illogical or eccentric about the use of the imperfective ходи́ть in Вчера́ мы ходи́ли в кино́. The difference between the perfective and imperfective aspects is based on a distinction between fulfilled and unfulfilled action. The logical fulfilment of the action of going to the cinema is *to arrive there and be there*, and this would be the implication of a perfective verb if used in this context (in fact, of course, to express the perfective idea of arriving the perfective пришли́ would be used; пошли́ would refer rather to setting out from the starting point).¹ What we normally mean when we say 'We went to the cinema' is that we paid a visit to the cinema, saw the film and went home. Since the point of the action is stated (в кино́), the perfective would emphasize the achievement of this point (the cinema), not the whole process of going *and* returning, which, as it were, 'undoes' the action of going *to*. This use of the imperfective past to refer to an action that has taken place, but whose effect has been cancelled by a subsequent 'undoing' of the action, is seen in other verbs involving moving, taking, shifting, etc. Compare, for example, the following pairs of sentences:

К вам заходи́л ваш брат.	Your brother came to see you (and went away again).
К вам зашёл ваш брат.	Your brother has come to see you (and he is here now).²
Я посыла́л его́ в магази́н.	I sent him to the shop (and now he's back).
Я посла́л его́ в магази́н.	I've sent him to the shop (he's still away).
Она́ брала́ э́ту кни́гу в библиоте́ке.	She borrowed this book from the library (she has taken it back).
Она́ взяла́ э́ту кни́гу в библиоте́ке.	She borrowed this book from the library (and still has it).

In these sentences the result of the action expressed by the imperfective verbs, though momentarily achieved, is not now 'in effect'.

If it is necessary to present a past round-trip action in a specifically perfective context (for example, as an action preceding or conditioning another), then the perfective verbs formed from the indeterminate with the prefix с- are used (сходи́ть, слета́ть, спла́вать, etc.). These verbs are also used to express the idea of 'going and coming back', etc., in the future and in imperatives. Their

---

[1] If colloquial usage allows Вчера́ мы пошли́ в кино́ to be used in the same sense as Вчера́ мы ходи́ли в кино́, this is simply an extension of the original terms of reference of the perfective verb (setting out for, or—as a result of going—being at the cinema). Cf. Forsyth (151).

[2] The perfective зашёл is, of course, not limited to this particular meaning: in other contexts—e.g. narrating a chain of events in the past—it might simply state that a visit was made. Similarly, the perfectives in the following examples may, depending on context, have other implications than those stated.

basic meaning is 'to go (etc.) and come back', usually, though not necessarily, within a short space of time (shortness of time is anyway a relative concept—for example, in Съе́здили и пожи́ли в Петербу́рге почти́ весь зи́мний сезо́н (Dostoyevsky, Бе́сы), 'They went to Petersburg and spent practically the whole winter there', the emphasis is not on shortness of time, but on the temporary nature of their sojourn). Сходи́ть, etc., are contextually more limited than the straightforward indeterminate imperfective in the past; they are more likely in contexts where the journey, etc., is carried out as a condition for or a preliminary to doing something else, or for some simple express purpose (for instance, to perform an errand). This element is evident in the following examples:

Он съе́здил домо́й,...привёз револьве́р. (Kuprin, Поеди́нок)	He drove home and brought (back) a revolver.
Он вошёл в свою́ камо́рку, уложи́л ...щенка́ на крова́ти,...сбе́гал сперва́ в коню́шню за соло́мой, пото́м в ку́хню за ча́шечкой молока́. (Turgenev, Муму́)	He went into his room, put the puppy on the bed, ran over to the stable for some straw and then to the kitchen for a cup of milk.

(*b*) Complexity of the second type is that in which a number of journeys are involved to fulfil some task of carrying, conveying, etc. (This, clearly, cannot affect verbs of individual motion: ходи́ть, е́здить, по́лзать, лета́ть, etc.)

Тётя Па́ша и шофёр ста́ли носи́ть всё это в дом. (Panova, Серёжа)	Auntie Pasha and the driver set about carrying all this into the house.

Here носи́ть implies that the number of things to be carried was too large to manage 'at one go', so a number of journeys had to be made. If, in the present case, what had to be carried was, say, a single large piece of furniture, which would be carried in in one journey, then ста́ли нести́ would be required.

...беле́ют в темноте́ свежеобстру́ганные сосёнки. На плеча́х таска́ли мы их из сосе́дней ро́щицы. (Nekrasov, В око́пах Сталингра́да)	The newly-stripped young pines gleam white in the darkness. We carted them (there) on our shoulders from the nearby thicket.

Here the carrying of the pines is presented as a complex action which involved various people in a number of journeys to and from the thicket.

(*c*) The third type of complexity is that resulting from an action that takes place on a number of occasions over a period of time. It is this that accounts for the use of indeterminate verbs to describe repeated, regular or habitual actions. The following are some examples:

Лу́нин мно́го раз лета́л над Кроншта́дтом. (Chukovsky, Балти́йское не́бо)	Lunin had flown over Kronstadt many times.
Он ча́сто е́здил по э́той доро́ге. (Chekhov, Сосе́ди)	He often travelled along this road.
Он ходи́л к ней раз в неде́лю.	He went to (see) her once a week.
17 раз в день в ата́ку ходи́ли. (Ostrovsky, Как закаля́лась сталь)	They went into the attack 17 times in a day.
Неуже́ли я здесь бу́ду жить?... Неуже́ли бу́ду ходи́ть по э́тим у́лицам, и е́здить в э́тих трамва́ях...? (Nikolayeva, Би́тва в пути́)	Am I really going to live here? Am I going to walk along these streets and ride in these trams?
Ува́ров лета́ет на «У-2». (Chukovsky, *op. cit.*)	Uvarov flies a U-2.
Ходи́л он не ско́ро, но больши́ми шага́ми. (Turgenev, Запи́ски охо́тника)	He did not walk quickly, but took big strides. (This occurs in a character-sketch.)

The distinction between determinate and indeterminate verbs is particularly clear in the following examples, where both a particular and a general or habitual action are referred to:

Он идёт бы́стро..., бу́дто не раз уже́ ходи́л здесь. (Nekrasov, В око́пах Сталингра́да)	He walks quickly, as though he has walked here many times before.
Мы пошли́ с ним, он вёл меня́, как во́дят ра́неных на войне́. (Aksyonov, Пора́, мой друг, пора́)	He and I set off. He led me along the way they lead wounded men in wartime.
Она́ шла так, как хо́дят на стадио́не, — спорти́вной, летя́щей по́ступью. (Nikolayeva, *op. cit.*)	She walked along the way people walk at the sports stadium, with a springing, athletic step.

Compare the similar switch of perspective in this example from *Anna Karenina*:

Впереди́ е́хала А́нна...В пе́рвую мину́ту ей [До́лли] показа́лось неприли́чно, что А́нна е́здит верхо́м.	In front rode Anna...At first it struck her [Dolly] as indecent for Anna to be riding on horse-back.

Е́хала refers to Anna's actual performance of the action of riding, е́здит to the fact that she rides *at all*.

When regular or habitual action is described, the indeterminate verb may tend to lose any strict idea of motion and indicate function rather than action (a characteristic which distinguishes it from the essentially dynamic determinate verbs). For example, Он хо́дит в шко́лу, Мы иногда́ хо́дим в теа́тр are hardly concerned with any actual idea of motion, but express the fact that the persons concerned *attend* or *frequent* the place mentioned (of course, the same kind of abstraction is evident in the English 'go to school', 'go to the theatre', in which 'go' has lost any actual motive implication).

In considering repeated and habitual actions, it must be remembered that they can in particular contexts be described by determinate verbs (see pp. 16–22, above). The indeterminate verbs are used only when the context allows an absolute view to be taken of the action as a collective whole.

We will now consider the uses of indeterminate verbs under the second main heading ('The action itself, not seen in application to any particular journey or line of movement'). These occur chiefly in general statements of various kinds (there might be grounds for including some of these under the rubric of 'repeated, regular, habitual actions', already mentioned), in statements about the capacity to perform the action in question ('to walk', 'to fly', etc.) and in statements where the action is envisaged merely as a set of physical motions unrelated to any practical application.

Among general statements, we find the indeterminate used in sentences such as:

Я люблю́ самолёты...Я хочу́ лета́ть. (Chukovsky, Балти́йское не́бо)	I love aeroplanes. I want to fly.
Кто вам дове́рил вози́ть люде́й?! Вы не шофёр! (Tendryakov, Уха́бы)	Who ever allowed you to drive people? You're no driver!

In neither of these sentences is any particular application of the movement envisaged; it is flying, driving anywhere at any time, not somewhere at a particular time, that is involved.

The indeterminate is the natural choice in general statements of fact such as:

То́лько су́мчатые живо́тные но́сят детёнышей в су́мке на животе́. (Slevich, Че́рез два океа́на)	Only marsupials carry their young in a pouch on their stomachs.

It is also used in contexts where the idea of 'to have ever done' is present:

[Вы] плáвали по Азóвскому мóрю? (Chukovsky, *op. cit.*)	Have you ever sailed on the Sea of Azov?
На истребителях летáли? (*Ibid.*)	Have you ever flown fighters?
Я летáл на «Дýгласе». (*Ibid.*)	I've flown in a Douglas.

Note the switch from indeterminate to determinate in the following exchange:

— Мнóго пришлóсь поéздить? — Éздить?...Вóсемь лет, могý сказáть, я тóлько и дéлал, что éхал, всё врéмя кудá-нибудь éхал. (Knorre, Пéрвый мéсяц)	'Did you do a lot of travelling?' 'Travelling? Why, for eight years I did nothing but travel, I was always going somewhere.'

Here the second speaker begins with the general notion of travelling (éздить), then pictures to himself the fact that he was constantly travelling, always on the way somewhere, and presents this in his reply as one uninterrupted progress (éхал). In a considered reply he might have said: 'Да, я мнóго éздил.'

Another kind of 'general' movement is any which is only observed vaguely and so cannot be defined in relation to any particular line of action. So, we find the indeterminate in

Он [Гéрманн] услы́шал незнакóмую похóдку: ктó-то ходи́л, ти́хо шáркая тýфлями. (Pushkin, Пи́ковая дáма)	He [Hermann] heard an unfamiliar step: someone was walking (about), softly scuffing their shoes.
Гдé-то хóдят. (Andreyev, Расскáз о семи́ повéшенных)	There are people walking (about) somewhere.

It is natural that the indeterminate verbs should be used to refer to the general capacity to walk, ride, etc., since, clearly, no particular context or application of the movement is envisaged. One says Ребёнок ужé пóлзает (The child is already crawling, i.e. has already acquired the capacity to crawl), Чéрез мéсяц больнóй ужé ходи́л без пáлки (In a month the sick man was walking (= could walk) without a stick), etc. When participles are used adjectivally to refer to people or things endowed with and characterized by an ability to fly, climb, etc., then again the indeterminate is used: летáющая тарéлка (flying saucer), летáющая лóдка (flying-boat), лáзящие растéния (climbing plants). Compare also нелетáющий in the air-force sense of 'grounded' (e.g. Вторáя эскадри́лья перешлá в разря́д нелетáющих, 'No. 2 Squadron was grounded' (Chukovsky, Балти́йское нéбо)).

Similarly, we find indeterminates used after умéть, учи́ться, etc., since, again, it is the capacity for movement, not its application, that is in mind: учи́ться éздить верхóм, умéть плáвать.

Context, however, can necessitate the use of determinate verbs in situations where something more precise than general capacity is involved. Compare the following exchange between a wounded man in a remote spot and his would-be rescuer:

— Ходи́ть не могу́. 'I can't walk.'
— ...Вы и ползти́ не мóжете? 'Can't you even crawl?'
(Chukovsky, *op. cit.*)

The wounded man refers to his general incapacity to walk (ходи́ть не могу́), but his companion, in using ползти́, is thinking of the fact that he has to get away and might *get along* by crawling— the *progressive* idea is introduced. This use of the determinate is regularly found when the ability or, more often, the inability to progress under particular circumstances is involved (another demonstration of the 'contextual' nature of determinate verbs). For example:

Конь...стал, ни вперёд, ни назáд, ни вбок — никудá...Нет, не мóжет идти́ конь. The horse stopped. Forward, back, sideways—it was impossible. No, the horse couldn't go (on).
(Kazakov, Ники́шкины тáйны)

Here, the horse's inability to go is due not to its own incapacity, but to the state of the terrain (it would be perfectly logical to say: 'Конь мóжет ходи́ть, но не мóжет идти́'). And when in *Three Sisters* Chebutykhin likens himself to a migratory bird, котóрая состáрилась, не мóжет летéть (that has grown old and cannot fly), he uses the determinate infinitive because he is thinking of the bird not as being generally incapable of flying (though here this may also be true), but as finding that it cannot fly in a particular context—when the time for migration comes.

Determinate verbs can also be used in expressions of general capacity. Mazon cites examples such as Он мóжет нести́ свобóдно четы́ре пу́да (He can easily carry 4 poods), Он мóжет идти́ и́ли éхать пять часóв без останóвки (He can walk or ride 5 hours without a break) (Mazon: 22). Such cases might be classed among the 'exemplary' uses of the determinate verbs discussed above (pp. 17–18)—there is an underlying suggestion of 'he can do this as the occasion demands', 'put him to the test and you would find that he can do this', and this encourages the use of the more graphic verb (нести́, etc.). It might be noted too that these statements refer to what the person in question can do 'at one go' and so the concern is precisely with 'singulative' action.

Finally, indeterminate verbs are used in contexts where the emphasis is on the action as a set of physical movements unrelated to any line of action. This is basically the same as their use to indicate capacity already mentioned, but there is usually the difference that in the present type of context the action is actual rather than potential. It was said at the beginning that the choice of determinate or indeterminate depends on the perspective in which the action is seen. If it is seen in the simple context of a straightforward action along a line, then the determinate is used. Complexity demands the use of the indeterminate, and so does the opposite extreme of no context at all. If the observer's focus is narrowed to such an extent that he sees only the subject and totally excludes his surroundings (which alone can provide the context for determinate action), then he is once more in the sphere of the indeterminate, e.g.

| Врачи́ веля́т побо́льше ходи́ть. Вот и хожу́. (Nekrasov, В родно́м го́роде) | The doctors say I must walk more, so here I am walking. |

| Серёжа нечаянно попа́л ного́й в колесо́, и 4 спи́цы вы́валились, но ничего́, велосипе́д всё е́здил. (Panova, Серёжа) | Seryozha accidentally stuck his foot in the wheel and 4 spokes fell out, but it didn't matter, the bike still went. |

The emphasis on the physical means of propulsion is seen in the following:

| Всё в поря́дке — сказа́л Сабу́ров, — за исключе́нием того́, что от генера́ла Проце́нко до полко́вника Ре́мизова прихо́дится по́лзать на животе́. (Simonov, Дни и но́чи) | 'Everything's fine', said Saburov, 'except for the fact that to get from General Protsenko to Colonel Remizov you have to crawl on your stomach.' |

Ходи́л in the following example also refers to the idea of performing the physical actions of walking:

| Когда́, вообража́я, что я иду́ на охо́ту,... я отпра́вился в лес, Воло́дя лёг на́ спину... и сказа́л мне, что бу́дто бы и он ходи́л. (Tolstoy, Де́тство) | When I went off into the wood making believe that I was going hunting, Volodya lay on his back and had me believe that he was coming too. |

When verbs of motion are used in senses other than those strictly concerned with physical action ('lead a life', 'bear a name', etc.), there can, of course, be no distinction between determinate and indeterminate action and so only one verb of the determinate/indeterminate pair is used for a given figurative sense (вести жизнь, носить имя, etc.). Although the verbs in such uses are more or less remote from their original senses denoting movement of various kinds, it is still usually clear enough why in certain instances the determinate and in others the indeterminate is used: the presence or absence of the *progressive* factor is the key.

For instance, the idea of progress—or activity involving 'passage through time' (Ward: 261)—is evident in contexts such as Работа идёт хорошо (The work is going/getting on well), Идут разговоры (Talks are taking place), Он ведёт распутную жизнь (He leads a dissolute life), Посол ведёт переговоры (The ambassador is conducting negotiations). The idea of pursuing a line of conduct (so, *progressive*) is clear in вести себя (behave), вести скучную, etc., жизнь (lead a dull, etc., life); of pursuing an activity in вести войну (wage war), вести кампанию (conduct a campaign); of keeping a progressive record of things in вести дневник (keep a diary), вести счёт (keep account), вести книги (keep books, accounts). Нести is used for the figurative 'bearing' of responsibilities, duties and moral burdens of various kinds: нести ответственность (bear responsibility), нести вахту (be on watch), нести дежурство (be on duty), нести последствия (bear the consequences), нести наказание (suffer punishment), нести вину (bear guilt). In the case of 'duty', 'watch', etc., the idea of conducting an activity, of keeping something going, might be claimed, while in the remainder the idea of being the *actual* load-bearer, or of carrying 'consequences', 'guilt', etc., through life with one (cf. *вести* жизнь), might be envisaged. The bearing of loads in buildings, etc., is also expressed by the 'actual' verb нести: Колонны несут всю тяжесть крыши (The columns bear the whole weight of the roof).

Of the indeterminate verbs that are used figuratively носить has most functions. Водить occurs in водить дружбу, знакомство (though it overlaps here with вести: вести дружбу, знакомство); ходить is used in ходить за больным ('look after a sick person'—here the idea of 'going round after' suggests an obviously complex activity), and in the sense of 'circulate' of coins, and also of rumours: ходит слух, 'there is a rumour (going round)'. The phrase идёт слух also exists, and, though there is no practical distinction in meaning, it is still perhaps possible to see a difference of idea—the idea of circulation (going round) in хо́дит слух and the idea of currency (in progress) in идёт слух (compare the use of идти́ in пье́са, фильм идёт, 'a play, film is on (= currently showing)'). Носи́ть is common in the sense of 'wear (habitually)' —носи́ть шля́пу, бо́роду, усы́ (wear a hat, a beard, a moustache, etc.)—reflecting the idea of non-progressive or complex carrying implicit in the indeterminate (cf. also ходи́ть (в чём-нибудь) used in the sense of 'wear', deriving from 'go around (in)'). Носи́ть is also used of permanent features, e.g. names (носи́ть и́мя, 'bear a name'; носи́ть зва́ние, 'bear a title'), and distinguishing marks, features (носи́ть при́знаки, 'bear the marks (of)'; носи́ть хара́ктер, 'possess the character (of)'). Not only are these things which are inevitably 'carried around' with one, but also, characteristically, they involve no *actual* load-bearing by the individual (in contrast to the figurative uses of нести́).

Apart from ходи́ть/идти́, води́ть/вести́, носи́ть/нести́, few other verbs of motion are used outside their basic meanings. Mention might be made of лезть (always with the idea of simple or directed motion in лезть не в своё де́ло, 'interfere in someone else's business', у него́ во́лосы ле́зут, 'his hair is falling out' (cf. other 'steady stream' natural phenomena like снег идёт), лезть на́ сте́ну, 'climb up the wall (in anger)'); and of гнать in the sense of 'distil', where progressive motion is evident enough.

BIBLIOGRAPHY

BIRKETT, G. A. *Modern Russian Course*. Methuen, London, 1937.
BORRAS, F. M. & CHRISTIAN, R. F. *Russian Syntax*. Oxford University Press, 1959.
FORSYTH, J. 'The Russian Verbs of Motion', *Modern Languages*. London, 1963, XLIV, no. 4, 147–52.
HINGLEY, R. & BINYON, T. J. *Russian: a Beginner's Course*. Allen and Unwin, London, 1962.
ISACHENKO, A. V. 'Глаголы движения в русском языке', *Русский язык в школе*. Moscow, 1961, no. 4, 12–16. (See also a detailed discussion of verbs of motion in the same author's *Die russische Sprache der Gegenwart*, Teil I, *Formenlehre*, pp. 419–42. Halle, 1962.)
MAZON, A. *Emplois des Aspects du Verbe Russe*. Paris, 1914.
RUZICKA, R. 'Einführung in die Flexion und Aspektbildung des russischen Verbs' in DAUM, E. & SCHENK, W., *Die russischen Verben*. Leipzig, 1954.
STILMAN, L. *Russian Verbs of Motion* (2nd ed.). King's Crown Press, New York, 1951.
UNBEGAUN, B. O. *Russian Grammar*. Oxford University Press, 1957.
VINOGRADOV, V. V. (ed.). *Грамматика русского языка*. Moscow, 1952–4.
WARD, D. *The Russian Language Today*. Hutchinson, London, 1965.

THE USE OF THE GENITIVE IN NEGATIVE CONSTRUCTIONS
by R. M. DAVISON

1. INTRODUCTION

When used in negative statements, most transitive Russian verbs offer a choice between the genitive case and the accusative for the direct object. The purpose of the present work is to indicate for the benefit of the English-speaking learner the criteria which operate in making this choice.

The 640 examples on which the conclusions are based have been drawn from prose written between 1944 and 1964.[1] In order to avoid the tendency to register only those instances which can be easily explained, approximately the first eighty occurrences of negative constructions in a given work have been taken as a random sample.

No account will be taken of verbs which take a direct object in the dative (e.g. мешáть, 'to hinder') or instrumental (e.g. прáвить, 'to rule, to drive') since they show no variation between positive and negative statements. The same is true of verbs which always take the genitive when used in the positive (e.g. боя́ться, 'to fear'), except that the use of such verbs in indirect negation through an infinitive will be mentioned (e.g. не боя́лся показáть свои́ чу́вства, 'he was not frightened to show his feelings' (Erenburg, Óттепель)). Excluded from consideration are: the invariable accusative in expressions of the type каки́е бы краси́вые словá он ни говори́л... (whatever fine words he might utter...); the invariable genitive in negative impersonal statements (e.g. не проéхало автомоби́ля, 'not a car went by'; не ви́дно дéрева, 'not a tree is to be seen'; не слы́шно пти́цы, 'not a bird is to be heard'); animate nouns with a genitive form for the accusative; ничегó (nothing).

---

[1] These examples have been used as a check on Restan's (see Bibliography) much larger collection: where there is no conflict and a clear indication is given I have accepted it, even though it is statistically unreliable.

Attention will be paid to verbs which, even in positive statements, are associated with both accusative and genitive for the direct object (e.g. ждать, 'to await'). Apart from negated transitive verbs, account will also be taken of other negative expressions (e.g. не надо, 'not necessary', нельзя, 'not permissible', не в силах, 'not within the power', не в состоянии, 'in no state', не прочь, 'not averse') and of negation transmitted through a dependent infinitive (e.g. он не начал читать книгу/книги, 'he did not begin to read the book'); these features will not, however, be treated separately since they fall under the heading of the general explanation.

2. W. A. MORISON'S THEORY

Previous treatments of this subject have nearly always contented themselves with stating that in certain circumstances the genitive is 'usually', 'often' or 'not infrequently' used. Thus, Restan (103) shows that 30 per cent of the plural nouns in his sample are in the accusative but gives no guidance as to which 30 per cent. This leaves the student wondering whether the particular plural noun which he is trying to use is one of the 30 per cent which are put into the accusative or one of the 70 per cent which, for some unspecified reason, are put into the genitive. For teaching purposes what is required is not merely a description but an explanation of usage.

The most cursory examination of the material will reveal that, on the basis either of lexical or grammatical criteria, or even on a combination of such criteria, it is very difficult to formulate any adequate explanation. Such explanations invariably leave a large number of examples where the grammatical and/or lexical features are similar but the case used varies between genitive and accusative. In view of this difficulty, attention has been turned by W. A. Morison (1959: 23 and 1964: 292–7) to the relationship between logical stress and grammatical form. His explanation has been presented in further detail by Dennis Ward (211–20). Although open to criticism both in presentation and in substance, Morison's explanation is of great value since it is neither lexically nor grammatically based.

The essence of Morison's theory is that the case to be used is determined by reference to the logical stress in the given context. If the logical stress of negation is directed to the verb, or to verb + object as a whole, i.e. to what is not *done* or does not *happen*, then the object is in the accusative; if the logical stress of negation is directed to the object, i.e. to that specific thing (rather than some other thing) which does not suffer some action or another, then the object is in the genitive. This may be illustrated in the following sentences.

Этот форт никогда никто не осаждал. (Paustovsky, Повесть о жизни)   No one had ever besieged this fort.

This sentence is preceded by two paragraphs describing the fort so that the reader is fully aware of what place is being discussed. The author is here stressing that a certain thing was not *done* to the fort, did not *happen* to it; he is negating the action of the verb. There is no question of any other fort being involved: so much has already been said about it that it can be assumed that the reader knows which fort is meant. The emphasis falls on what did or did not happen to it, hence the accusative case.

Антощенко мельком посмотрел на нас, неграмотных, ловко вбросил шашку в ножны и сказал:
— А эту шваль я и смотреть не желаю.
(Paustovsky, Повесть о жизни)

Antoshchenko gave us illiterates a quick glance, neatly threw his sword into its scabbard and said: 'I don't even want to set eyes on that rabble.'

In the direct speech it is quite clear to the reader who are the characters involved: Antoshchenko and the rabble. What is new and of interest is Antoshchenko's attitude to the rabble: what will he want to do to them? Will he want to feed them, pay them or flog them? Will he want to look at them? The answer is that he does not want even this to be done: he does not want even to set eyes on them. We know who they are and this is what he does not want to happen to them, hence the accusative case.

...чтобы оба германских государства взяли на себя обязательство не производить, не использовать, не приобретать атомное оружие... (Правда, 6. IX. 64)

...that both German states take upon themselves the obligation not to produce, not to use, not to acquire atomic weapons...

This example needs no further explanation since the succession of infinitives makes it obvious that it is to the negating of these that the author's attention is directed; hence, again, the accusative case.

Интере́сная же́нщина, в Москве́ я тако́й не встре́тил. (Erenburg, Óттепель)	An interesting woman; I didn't meet any like her in Moscow.

Here the implication is that although the writer did meet certain women in Moscow (i.e. the force of the verb 'the meeting' is not negated) he did not meet such a woman as this. The sense is 'I met no such woman in Moscow', where 'such' is negated but 'met' is not. The negation is directed to the object, which is, therefore, in the genitive case.

Понима́ла она́ и то, что не смо́жет измени́ть уже́ всем я́сного реше́ния. (Nikolayeva, Би́тва в пути́)	She also understood that she would not be able to change a decision which was already clear to everybody.

Doubtless she could change all sorts of things; perhaps she could even change some decisions; but not this particular type of decision. It is *the decision*, i.e. the object of the verb, which cannot be changed, which is negated and which is, therefore, in the genitive case.

Мы по́льзовались его́ услу́гами и дара́ми, никогда́ не принима́я в расчёт его́ нужд и печа́лей. (Leonov, Ру́сский лес)	We made use of his services and talents but never took into account his needs and sorrows.

The very construction of this sentence directs attention to the two pairs of nouns: услу́гами и дара́ми on the one hand and нужд и печа́лей on the other. The general sense is: various things were taken into account, but *not* his needs and sorrows. Clearly the verb is not negated, since account *was* taken of certain things indicated in the first half of the sentence; the negation is limited to and directed at the last two nouns of the sentence, which are, therefore, in the genitive.

За ва́ше подро́бное сообще́ние остаётся то́лько поблагодари́ть вас. Но вы не рассказа́ли гла́вного... (Azhayev, Далеко́ от Москвы́)	It remains only to thank you for your detailed report. But you have not told us the main thing...

Apparently the person referred to has related a great deal. It would, therefore, be unreasonable to attach the negation to рассказа́ли. The negation is directed to that thing which did not suffer the process of being related: 'the main thing'.

The main criticism to be made of the presentation of the Morison theory is that both Morison and Ward have worked on the assumption that it is true and have then shown what the genitive/accusative distinction must mean. Whichever case is used it is nearly always possible to apply Morison's theory and produce a plausible justification for the use of that case. This may sound to the Hegelian like the definition of a grammarian's paradise, but in fact the explanation tends to rely on the assumption of its own correctness to prove its truth. The Morison argument is: the noun is in the genitive case, therefore the stress of negation is on the noun; or the noun is in the accusative case, therefore the stress of negation is on the verb or on the verb plus noun. To prove that the explanation is correct, however, every example from a representative selection of negative constructions should be considered in its full context in order that an attempt may be made to assess, independently of any indication which might be given by the case of the object, where the logical stress of negation falls. Even with these safeguards the analysis of examples is a perilous procedure; without them, error is almost assured and this error is of a variety which is troublesome to detect. For instance, Ward (217) quotes from Erenburg:

Он [не ви́дел] [Со́ни].	He did not see Sonya.

The square brackets are a graphic indication of Ward's analysis of this sentence, which is: '*He did not see Sonya* (but he may have seen others).' Since Ward is re-quoting Restan's examples it is possible by reference to Restan (97) to trace this sentence back to Óттепель. The context is:

[Со́ня] прошла́ к себе́ и, не зажига́я све́та, се́ла на крова́ть. Ей хоте́лось хотя́ бы на мину́ту оста́ться одно́й... В ко́мнату ти́хо вошёл Са́вченко. Он не ви́дел Со́ни и, протяну́в ру́ку, косну́лся её плеча́, о́бнял, стал целова́ть. (Erenburg, Óттепель)	[Sonya] went across to her own room and, not putting on the light, sat down on the bed. She wanted to be on her own if only for a minute... Savchenko quietly came into the room. He did not see Sonya and, stretching out his hand, touched her shoulder, embraced her and began to kiss her.

This seems to rule out the idea of Savchenko seeing any others because there was no one there and if there had been he is unlikely to have seen them because the light was not on. That the emphasis is on what did or did not happen, on the different sense impressions (which ought, according to Morison, to produce the accusative), is indicated by the succession of verbs at the end of the sentence under discussion. There can be no question in the reader's mind of any stress being given to Sonya as opposed to somebody else—there is no one else. All of the stress is devoted to what happens, to the verbs. This example is not in accordance with Morison's theory and is to be explained by the use of the verb видеть (see pp. 42–3).

Two further examples re-quoted by Ward (217) are of interest: (*a*) [не] [снимая фуражку] and (*b*) [не скинув] [фуражки] (not taking off his cap). From the disposition of the brackets Ward's analysis can be deduced as follows: (*a*) 'What did he not do? He did not take off his cap.' (*b*) 'What did he not take off? His cap.' It may well be that these analyses are correct when the sentences are taken in their full context, but Ward does not justify himself by context. Regarding the quotations objectively and out of context it is impossible to detect any difference in logical stress unless it is assumed from the start that Morison's theory is true. It is only rarely that a manifestly absurd result is obtained by applying the theory, e.g.

коровой...не дававшей молока...   a cow not giving milk...
    (Turgenev, Записки охотника)

A Morison type of analysis here would lead to the conclusion that the cow did not give *milk*, though it may have given something else. (It is justifiable to take a nineteenth-century example since Morison acknowledges no historical limitations.) A further example:

Он снова взял её руку и, поце-   He took her hand again, kissed it and
ловав, оставил в своей. Софья   held it in his own. Sof'ya Pavlovna did
Павловна руки не отняла, но сухо   not take her hand away but said
сказала... (Il'ina, Возвращение)   dryly...

Is the reader to conclude that Sof'ya removed, not her hand, but perhaps her foot? (These examples can be accounted for in different ways. See pp. 45–6.)

So far, remarks have been confined to criticisms of existing presentations of the Morison theory. However, there are some observations to be made on its substance.

It does not concern itself in any detail with sentences where the logical stress of negation appears to fall equally on the verb and on the object. Ward just mentions this point when he says (220): 'It may also be that the occasional unexpected use of one case instead of the other occurs in "marginal" instances, where the difference between the two meanings is very small or negligible in the particular context.' An attempt will be made below to show that criteria for choice do exist in such contexts.

A weakness is apparent also in the Ward/Morison discussion of negative clauses with a predicative instrumental. Ward says (219): '...one would not expect to find the genitive in such a sentence as Я не считаю э́то обязательным *I do not consider this obligatory*, for the emphasis is not on *what* is not considered obligatory but on what is not *done*. The genitive is not impossible, however, in such structures, for if one says Э́то я считаю обязательным, а э́того я не считаю обязательным *This I consider obligatory but this I do not consider obligatory*, the emphasis in the second clause is not on what is not *done* but on *what* is not considered obligatory.' Morison says (1964: 295): '...it is natural that "I do not find Russian difficult" should be "Ja ne nachožu russky jazyk trudnym" if the logical stress is on "not finding it difficult"; if the meaning were "I don't find *Russian* difficult (but I do find, e.g. *Chinese* difficult)", one would expect neg. gen. "russkogo jazyka".' It is interesting that Ward resorts to 'if one says' and makes up his own example to illustrate genitive usage and Morison tells the reader what to expect if the theory is true. Neither writer provides an actual example of a genitive in these circumstances which would illustrate an established usage. In his collection of examples of negative usage Restan has twelve clauses with a predicative instrumental and only in one is the genitive used: a consideration of the full context of this exception indicates that it is not one of the type—devised by Ward and expected by Morison—which make a strong distinction between the direct objects of the verb. Restan's sample is small but its clear indications are supported by most who have studied the construction. Unless a substantial and representative body of examples with the genitive is produced from an original source it would seem proper to exclude this construction from Morison's theory, and regard it as in all probability one which requires the accusative.

In considering the same example—э́то я считаю обязательным, а э́того я не считаю обязательным—from a different standpoint, Ward points out that in 'this sentence the word-order serves to contrast one "this" with another "this". Such devices of contrast and emphasis...can serve the same ends as the negative genitive / negative accusative contrast.' If this is true and if Morison is right, then it would be expected that in a clause where inversion occurs the object would usually be in the genitive. However, this is not so (see Restan: 99). This does not, of course, disprove Morison's theory but does indicate the need of some supplementary explanation (see pp. 54–6).

Finally, it is both necessary and proper to accept that a number of examples of negative constructions cannot be adequately explained. As Restan and Safarewiczowa have shown, this is a field in which, even if stabilization has perhaps been reached by now, practice has changed over recent years; 'this would account for the occasional dubious use of one case or the other' (Ward: 220). It is no adverse criticism of a theory that it takes account of the fact that native writers of the language do not necessarily know what they are doing. A category of inexplicable examples serves as an expansion joint to absorb the strains arising when a changing phenomenon is caught within the limitations of a static theory.

Morison himself admits that certain examples require further consideration in the light of his theory (1964: 296), and deliberately confronts himself with a sentence which seems to go against it:

...он...оглянулся, но не увидел мачехи, а снова услышал её возглас... (Gor'ky, Жизнь Матвея Кожемякина)

He looked round but did not see his stepmother; but he heard her cry again...

Since Morison does not refer to the context of this sentence to justify his analysis, it seems reasonable, ignorant of the context, to offer an alternative analysis in the light of his theory. The information available within the sentence all points to an emphasis on the subject's sense impressions. The word снова indicates that he had already heard one cry; её implies that he knew whose cry it was. Therefore, when he looked round, he expected to *see* (because he *looked* he would expect to *see*, not *hear*, and in any case he could hear her without looking round) his stepmother, but instead of seeing something he heard something. The logical stress is on what did or did not happen and should, by Morison's theory, lead to the accusative. Of course, to quote Morison (1964: 297), 'the statement using the negative genitive may be taken as answering the question "*Whom* didn't he see when he glanced around?" Answer: "*His stepmother*." (But once again he heard her exclamation)', but this seems to fly in the face of the evidence from the sentence. Again, the 'rule' for the use of видеть (see pp. 42–3) provides a more plausible explanation. The attempt to explain every example which occurs is laudable but misguided. There are instances where the theory will not work without stretching the imagination; if the theory is applied to a representative sample of negative constructions, it becomes apparent that many of these instances have certain features in common (see section 3 below).

Despite its weaknesses, however, Morison's theory is still the only one which attempts an explanation, rather than a mere description, of usage. If care is taken in applying it to see that the reader's decision on the position of the logical stress is determined by the context and not by the use of one case or the other, then it will still be found that the theory works in an impressive number of examples. In view of this, it is worth seeing if the theory can be modified or expanded so that one is not obliged to explain by it either what can better be explained otherwise or what is truly inexplicable.

3. MODIFICATIONS OF MORISON'S THEORY

It was mentioned above that when Morison's theory is applied to a representative sample of negative constructions it is found that, although there are few which will not fit at all, there are more where considerable doubt arises. Examination of these two inconvenient categories reveals a certain pattern. There is, of course, still a residue of inexplicable examples outside the new pattern.

A. *ви́деть, говори́ть, замеча́ть, понима́ть, знать*[1]

In the first place it is noticeable that certain verbs are associated with the genitive in negative constructions in a very high percentage of the cases where they are used. These verbs are ви́деть, говори́ть, замеча́ть, понима́ть, знать, together with compounds of some of them. For *verba sentiendi* in general Restan (100) gives an accusative frequency of 19·8 per cent as against 32·8 per cent with other negated verbs. Restriction of the sample to the verbs listed above produces the appreciably lower accusative figure (from the present collection) of 3·5 per cent (excluding uses with этого, 'this/that'). This low figure does not in itself indicate that Morison's theory is wrong, or even partially wrong: there is no absolute reason why genitive/accusative proportions should be the

---

[1] Indications for the genitive given in sections A–F are to be disregarded if не is directly associated with the object (see pp. 56–7).

same across different lexical categories, though one would expect the proportions to be the same since Morison's theory is not lexically based. However, a detailed examination of the individual examples shows that in an appreciable number of cases the use of one of these verbs leads to a genitive despite logical stress indications for an accusative. They can, therefore, be regarded as requiring the genitive.

видеть

See the examples and analyses from Erenburg (p. 38 above) and Gor'ky (p. 41 above): both of these can be accounted for with less strain if видеть is regarded as requiring the genitive.

говорить

...приписав себе все те слова, которых она Клавдии не сказала, а придумала потом.
(Il'ina, Возвращение)

...attributing to herself all those words which she had not said to Claudia but had thought up later.

There is only one direct object involved here—'the words'—which suffers a variety of actions. The emphasis is on the negation or otherwise of these actions, which might be expected to lead to the accusative. The genitive которых is all the more surprising since it is the object also of the positive verb придумала.

замечать

Чохов буркнул в ответ что-то непонятное, не очень довольный обращением к нему на «ты» и вообще всей манерой Воробейцева. Но Воробейцев как будто и не заметил хмурого выражения лица Чохова и продолжал...
(Kazakevich, Дом на Площади)

In reply Chokhov mumbled something incomprehensible; he was not very pleased with Vorobeytsev's familiar mode of address or with his whole manner. But Vorobeytsev seemed not to notice Chokhov's gloomy expression and went on...

In the sentence of interest the expression on Chokhov's face is no more than an extension of what the reader already knows about him. The new element in the sentence, which takes the emphasis, is Vorobeytsev's lack of response to Chokhov's irritation: the reader learns now what he did not do ('notice') and what he did do ('go on'). This analysis points to an accusative by Morison's theory supported by the intensive negation (и, 'even') with the verb.

понимáть

— А мóжет, он и сам старовéр? — пошутил Синцóв.
— Сáм-то он партийный, — дáже не пожелáв понять шýтки, сказáл Караýлов...
(Simonov, Живы́е и мёртвые)

'Perhaps he's an old-believer himself?' joked Sintsov.
'No, he's a party man', said Karaulov, not even wanting to see the joke...

It is clear that the object of discussion is the joke and that it does not require attention. The negation of the verbs is emphasized by the use of дáже. These features point to an accusative on the basis of logical stress of negation.

Это он понимáл и дéйствовал своим крáсным карандашóм без колебáний. Не понимáл он другóго: как...
(Simonov, Живы́е и мёртвые)

He understood this and used his red pencil unhesitatingly. The other thing he did not understand was how...

Everything in these sentences directs the logical stress to the contrast between the two actions. This might be expected to lead to the accusative.

знать

Родзаéвский знал то, чегó не знал Евсéев... (Il'ina, Возвращéние)

Rodzayevsky knew what Yevseyev did not know...

The distinction is between knowing and not knowing the one thing at issue. The emphasis of negation falls on the action, not on the object. Accusative is indicated by Morison's theory.

B. *э́того*

The second feature which seems always to require the genitive is the occurrence of the pronoun 'this/that' (i.e. э́того). The sample used for the present work gives just under 7 per cent accusative frequency for э́то. Examination of the examples shows that often a genitive is used against the indications given by a consideration of logical stress. Such indications with this pronoun are very frequently in the direction of the accusative since it is so often used to refer 'to something just previously mentioned or indicated' (Borras and Christian: 262).

Капитáну Воробéйцеву америкáнские солдáты понрáвились. Они были стяжáтелями, но не скрывáли э́того.
(Kazakevich, Дом на плóщади)

Captain Vorobeytsev liked the American soldiers. They were acquisitive but did not hide the fact.

...которые стремились к тому же самому, но открыто этого никогда не выражали. (Kazakevich, Дом на площади)	...who were aiming at the same thing but never expressed it openly.
То, что ты любишь Зину больше других, — твоё дело. Но показывать этого не нужно. (Il'ina, Возвращение)	The fact that you love Zina more than the others is your business. But there is no need to show it.

It is evident even from the limited context given that the emphasis in each case is on what was not *done*. By Morison's theory this should lead to the accusative.

In the present collection of examples, where this pronoun is used with one of the verbs mentioned above (видеть, говорить, etc.), there is no instance of accusative usage. In addition, there is serious doubt in more than 50 per cent of such cases as to whether an adequate explanation of the genitive (этого) could be offered in terms of Morison's theory, e.g.

Допросив, их обычно отпускали, одним сказав, куда примерно надо идти, а другим ничего не сказав, потому что не знали этого сами. (Simonov, Живые и мёртвые)	Having questioned them, they usually sent them away. They told some roughly where to go but told others nothing because they did not know [this] themselves.
Она начала неуверенно надевать перчатки, но Евсеев сделал вид, что не заметил этого, и быстро сказал... (Il'ina, Возвращение)	She started, hesitantly, to put her gloves on, but Yevseyev pretended not to notice [this] and quickly said...

Note: An exception to the use of этого (rather than это) is in negative clauses with a predicative instrumental, e.g. это я не считаю обязательным (see above, p. 40).

C. *Parts of the body (Reflexive)*

The third feature which appears to be indiscriminately associated with the genitive is more complex: when the object of a negated transitive verb refers to parts of the body of the subject of the verb, then that object is in the genitive, e.g.

Он снова взял её руку и, поцеловав, оставил в своей. Софья Павловна руки не отняла, но сухо сказала... (Il'ina, Возвращение)	He took her hand again, kissed it and held it in his own. Sof'ya Pavlovna did not take her hand away but said dryly...

It was indicated on p. 39 above that a Morison-type analysis of this sentence produces a somewhat curious result.

| Но Веретёнников не поднял руки. | ...but Veretennikov did not raise his |
| (Kazakevich, Дом на площади) | hand. |

D. *Unstressed zero quantity*

The fourth genitive requirement can be described, for reasons which will become apparent, as 'unstressed zero quantity'. Restan (102), amongst others, has pointed out that where there is a partitive sense the object is in the genitive, e.g.

| — Что же это вы, ребята, водки | What's the matter, lads? Why aren't |
| не пьёте? (Il'ina, Возвращение) | you drinking vodka? |

This is perhaps not very surprising. It is not, however, sufficient as an explanation. There occur also constructions in which the genitive is used in contradiction to Morison; in some of these a partitive genitive would not certainly be used in the positive and in others it quite certainly would not. The particular meaning expressed by a partitive genitive is more frequently required in the negative than in the positive. Ward (212) has mentioned the category of zero quantity in connection with the obligatory use of the genitive with, for example, нет, не было, не будет (there is/are not, there was/were not, there will not be). The qualification 'unstressed' must be introduced for obvious reasons. Where stress is laid on the total absence of the object the genitive would in any case be expected in accordance with Morison's theory; this view is supported by the almost exclusive use of the genitive in association with expressions of intense negation (ни, и, никакой, 'not a...'), i.e. in expressions of *stressed* zero quantity. It seems that in other instances, such as those mentioned here, there is an attempt to convey with precision the total absence of the object without laying great emphasis on this absence. Perhaps the difference can be conveyed in English: 'it *didn't* raise any alarm' as opposed to 'it raised *no* alarm (at all)'. There is a difference of emphasis here —requiring different cases by Morison's theory—though in each instance the alarm is totally absent and, as will be shown below, the genitive would in fact be used in each instance in Russian.

The present view of the matter is perfectly expressed in Jakobson's words when he says (257) that the genitive indicates 'das Nichtvorhandensein des Gegenstandes im Sachverhalte der Aussage' (the absence of the object, in the context of the statement). However, he goes on to make important qualifications about stress which lead him to a position somewhat removed from the present one. The usage indicated here probably also lies behind the concrete/abstract or specific/general opposition which has been seen by many as an important factor in the matter of case choice. It seems reasonable to suggest also that the obligatory genitives in expressions such as не обращать внимания, не оказывать влияния, have survived not simply as petrified constructions but because they also reflect a usage which still has meaning, i.e. 'not to pay any attention', 'not to have any influence'. Examples:

Может быть, она мне напишет? Тогда я поеду в Пензу. А если не напишет, ни за что не поеду, вообще не возьму отпуска... (Erenburg, Оттепель)	Perhaps she will write to me. In that case I will go to Penza. But if she doesn't write, I won't go for anything. I won't take any leave at all...

The emphasis throughout is on the various happenings, i.e. on the verbs. 'отпуск' might, therefore, be expected to be in the accusative; the genitive seems, whilst not removing any of the stress from the verbs, to convey the sense 'any leave'.

Он на себя не похож, не ломается, не изрекает афоризмов. (Erenburg, Оттепель)	He isn't like himself, he isn't putting on airs, he isn't uttering any aphorisms.

The construction of the sentence, with its succession of negations, suggests that in each instance the whole expression is being negated: (i) the adjective, (ii) the verb, (iii) the verb+object. In item (iii) this would lead to the accusative by Morison's theory. The genitive indicates 'any aphorisms'.

Лёля пригласила всех присутствующих в гости, предупредив при этом не без задней мысли, что подарков можно не приносить. (Antonov, Избранное)	Lelya invited everybody who was there and at the same time told them, not without ulterior motive, that it would be all right not to bring [any] presents.

Once again, the construction of the sentence is such that emphasis is laid on the verb and an accusative might be expected by Morison's theory.

Раз база не берёт огурцов, мы вынуждены силосовать их. (Правда, 10. IX. 64)	If the depot does not take the cucumbers, we are compelled to store them.

The discussion preceding this quotation has concerned the difficulties of getting shops and distributors to take cucumbers, and someone has said: 'Не принимают огурцы' (they are not taking the cucumbers), i.e. we are talking about our cucumbers—as is well known to everybody—and it is a question of whether they do or do not take them. This usage is quite consistent with Morison. In the present quotation it is still a question of taking or not taking (rather than of, say, cucumbers as opposed to tomatoes); the emphasis remains the same and so should the case, if Morison is completely right. The case change seems to indicate a slight difference in the scope of the object; 'if they don't take *any* cucumbers (not just ours)'.

| ...на́ши войска́, преодоле́в ожесточённое сопротивле́ние проти́вника, шту́рмом овладе́ли... на́ши войска́ овладе́ли населёнными пу́нктами... не встре́тив осо́бого сопротивле́ния проти́вника. | ...our troops overcame vicious opposition from the enemy and took by storm...our troops took the centres of population...without meeting any especial opposition from the enemy. |

(Kazakevich, Дом на пло́щади)

Since the object ('enemy opposition') is repeated, the attention is automatically directed to what did or did not happen to the opposition. Such emphasis would require the accusative by Morison's theory. The genitive signifies 'any...opposition', without altering the emphasis of negation.

E. *боя́ться, хоте́ть, жела́ть, etc.*

Certain verbs, e.g. боя́ться, хоте́ть, жела́ть, etc., even when used in positive statements, are associated, either invariably or frequently, with the genitive case. When such verbs directly govern an object in a negative construction they always take the genitive case, e.g.

| — Нет, не жела́ю я и́хнего насле́дства. | No, I don't want their legacy. |

(Kazakevich, Дом на пло́щади)

There is in the present collection only a small number of examples of such verbs governing a direct object through a dependent infinitive and no statistical information on this particular construction seems to be available elsewhere. Of the twelve instances in the present sample, seven have the object in the accusative. Such a distribution in a small sample gives no indication of usage. One point is, however, remarkable. Constructions of indirect negation through an infinitive with verbs other than the type being discussed here can usually be accounted for by Morison's theory with the modifications indicated above. For such constructions Restan (94) gives an accusative frequency of 60·1 per cent (as opposed to 21·2 per cent for direct negation). It might be expected that even in indirect negation бояться, хотеть, etc., would maintain their genitive preference, but the sample, admittedly inadequate, indicates a 58·3 per cent accusative frequency. This is close to Restan's figure of 60·1 per cent, which excludes verbs of the type discussed here. It may be true, therefore, to say that these verbs behave like any others when used in indirect negation, though the evidence is far from conclusive. Examples:

Ей ничем не хотелось портить спокойной, радостной и дорогой ей дружбы.
(Nikolayeva, Битва в пути)

She did not want in any way to spoil a quiet, pleasant friendship which she valued.

...не боялся показать свои чувства... (Erenburg, Оттепель)

...he was not frightened to show his feelings...

Она не желала видеть эту слезу.
(Il'ina, Возвращение)

She did not want to see this tear.

F. *Equal logical stress of negation*

There exists in Russian a type of negative clause in which as much logical stress lies on the negation of the total action as lies on the negation of the object to which the action refers. In such instances it is clearly impossible to determine case by Morison's method. It appears that other factors come into play.

If the negated verb is in the form of a gerund or participle, the object will be in the genitive, e.g.

Молодой инженер обходился с Тополевым предупредительно, ни в чём не проявляя своих прав начальника отдела.
(Azhayev, Далеко от Москвы)

The young engineer was cautious in his dealings with Topolev; he in no way made it felt that he was head of the department.

The interest here is as much on what the engineer did or did not do in general as on what in particular he did not show or make felt. The question might be asked: 'How did the engineer treat Topolev?' The answer would be: 'In this way' or 'Not in this way', i.e. 'не [проявляя своих прав].' The negation of the entire bracketed section should lead to the accusative for the object, but since the reader does not know *what* he did not show, a genitive may equally be expected. The gerundial form of the verb appears to be the deciding factor in such cases.

Не скрывая своей радости, Воробейцев так же хлопнул Чохова по плечу... (Kazakevich, Дом на площади)	Not hiding his joy, Vorobeytsev also slapped Chokhov on the shoulder...

As in the preceding example, the negative clause as a whole serves as an answer to the question: 'How did he do whatever he did?' It is, therefore, negated as a whole. But the reader is equally interested in what he was not concealing, since it has not been mentioned before. The negation of the whole clause would require the accusative, the negation of the object concealed, the genitive. The gerund tips the balance to the genitive.

If the negation is transmitted through an infinitive, the object will be in the accusative, e.g.

И всё-таки эти мысли...не смогли заслонить от него тот факт, что... (Kazakevich, Дом на площади)	And yet these thoughts could not conceal from him the fact that...

The interest is equally divided between the general effect of the thoughts and the precise thing which they were or were not capable of obscuring. Either genitive or accusative is indicated on Morison's criteria. The infinitive seems to decide the issue in such cases.

If the object is a noun ending, in the nominative, in -а or -я then the accusative is used, e.g.

...если не получит гусиный генерал гусиную армию под начало! (Nikolayeva, Битва в пути)	...if a foolish general is not given command of a foolish army!
Но никаким разговором не заменишь горячую работу. (Azhayev, Далеко от Москвы)	But talk is no substitute for hard work.

Clauses will, of course, occur in which the logical stress of negation is equal and the choice criteria offered here conflict. In such circumstances the hierarchy of effectiveness seems to be that gerund or participle prevails over noun in -а/-я or infinitive. For example, gerund prevailing over noun in -а:

Он сидел за столом, не снимая скуфейки, пил чай... (Paustovsky, Повесть о жизни)	He was sitting at the table drinking tea, without having taken off his skull-cap...

and gerund prevailing over infinitive (where, as frequently happens, it is the infinitive and not the gerund which is negated):

...стараясь не уронить лёгких, как воздух, цветочков.
(Antonov, Избранное)

...trying not to drop the little flowers, which were as light as air.

There is, of course, no guarantee that in sentences with equal stress there will be present any of the criteria for case choice mentioned above. In such instances the genitive is used, e.g.

Климович слышал голоса, но не разбирал слов.
(Simonov, Живые и мёртвые)

Klimovich heard voices but could not make out the words.

Генерал Куприянов не любил продолжительных разговоров.
(Kazakevich, Дом на площади)

General Kupriyanov did not like protracted conversations.

Это впечатление не ослабляло значительности речи.
(Paustovsky, Повесть о жизни)

This impression did not reduce the significance of the speech.

It may be objected that the application of Morison's theory to the sentences quoted in this section on equal stress does not lead to nonsense and that, therefore, the category of equal stress is unnecessary. This may be true for the analysis of existing sentences, but the concern in the present work is to provide a teaching aid which will help the student to compose sentences which do not yet exist and in which he may be unable to distinguish any stress difference in what he wants to say.

G. *Inexplicable uses*

It was mentioned above (p. 41) that a category of inexplicable examples should be included in any account of the negative genitive. That it exists will be disputed by few. That it should exist is perhaps not so apparent.

Russian has a long history of using the genitive as the direct object of transitive verbs in positive statements, notably with *verba sentiendi* (see Lépissier on this feature in Church Slavonic). Further indecision is brought about by the long-established use of the genitive form for the accusative in certain instances (i.e. masculine singular and all plurals of animate nouns). In the spoken language, an additional factor is the identity between accusative and genitive singular forms of words with unstressed final -o, e.g. слово/слова (word). Then there is the question of verbs like ждать (to await) which can even now take a genitive direct object in positive uses. Such a combination of factors has brought about a situation where it is very difficult to regard as wrong any use of either case in negative constructions. A survey of a large collection of examples, such as Restan's with over two thousand, will provide a quotation to confound virtually any theory which could be devised. It might, for instance, be thought that the use with a negative of ничего́ (nothing) rather than ничто́ provided a watertight rule; but Restan (99) provides the following example:

Ничто́ челове́к так глубо́ко не пря́чет, как мечту́.'   Man hides away nothing so deeply as his daydreams.
(Paustovsky, Золота́я Ро́за)

This is such a manifest freak of usage that it can be discounted for all practical purposes. It does, however, illustrate the point that one case or the other with a negative can rarely be said to be wrong with the same conviction that would be used in condemning, say, *Я не зна́ю э́тому челове́ку (I do not know to this man). The use of a particular case in particular circumstances, however they are defined, may show a 99·9 per cent frequency but, remote though it may be, the possibility still exists of using the other case without making complete nonsense.

It seems that the only categories of 100 per cent consistency on recorded examples are (*a*) certain idioms, e.g. не обраща́ть внима́ния (to pay no attention), (*b*) uses with никако́й (no). This is probably a piece of good luck rather than anything else: if someone ever chose to write, for example, он не обраща́ет внима́ние на э́то (he pays no attention to that), it would undoubtedly, by present standards, be wrong but not in the same degree as if a dative were used for the direct object with this verb. Whatever the degree of probability for a particular case, then, it is in the end almost always possible to use either case without committing an enormity.

In addition to this must be considered the fact that, if the present formulation of criteria for choice is correct, the choice itself is often difficult to make. This arises from the subtle nature of Morison's idea about varying impact of logical stress of negation. That most of the inexplicable examples are genitives seems to indicate a tendency still to regard this as the first choice, from which deviations to the accusative are justified only in special circumstances; such a view is reflected in the use of the genitive with equal logical stress where there are none of the special indications for case choice mentioned in section F above. It is, therefore, 'easier' to use the genitive than the accusative; the result will usually be a sentence which still makes sense and is offensive grammatically only to someone who is keenly aware of the distinctions between the cases. Whichever case is used, if the rule disregarded is Morison's basic formulation the consequence may simply be a sentence which means something slightly different from what was intended, and this may well not matter very much, e.g.

Познакόмились они год назáд.   They met a year ago. Lena will not
Лéна не забýдет того́ вéчера...   forget that evening...
    (Erenburg, Óттепель)

Does any possible distinction on grounds of logical stress between this use and Лéна не забýдет тот вéчер really matter? This is not, of course, to say that such a distinction does not exist. The point is that its subtlety and frequent lack of importance are likely to lead to uncertainty of usage.

A third factor contributing to the difficulties of the problem is that, whatever the 'correct' usage may be, it is scarcely established. It has been shown (by Safarewiczowa and Restan) that accusative frequency has increased with the passage of time. However, there are still great individual differences between authors writing within a limited period (see Restan: 106–7). The reader has before his eyes examples of such widely differing usage that his own is bound to be somewhat insecure. His subconscious appreciation of what is happening may take him often, or less often, near to the rules indicated here, but until usage is established, i.e. until accusative frequency across a representative sample of authors shows—other things being equal—little individual difference between the authors, he is likely to make a fair number of 'wrong' choices.

The fourth aggravation of the problem is the absence of any satisfactorily detailed normative pronouncement, with the partial exception of the work of Morison and Ward. It is, of course, true that a normative pronouncement can properly be made only when usage is fairly well settled, but if it is made at an advanced stage of development of the grammatical feature it can help greatly in settling the usage.

In view, therefore, of
   (*a*) the basic possibility of using either case without gross offence,

(*b*) the subtlety of some of the possible criteria for choice,
(*c*) the fluid state of the phenomenon, and
(*d*) the absence of any widely known and accepted criteria for choice,

it is only proper to allow for a fair number of examples which go against such rules as it may be possible to formulate.

4. MINOR ASPECTS OF THE PROBLEM

A. *Inversion*

It was indicated above (pp. 40–1) that there is apparently a contradiction between Morison's theory and statistical evidence on the matter of case choice where inversion occurs. If it is true that in inversion the word placed in an abnormally advanced position in the clause gains in emphasis, then, according to Morison, the genitive would be expected for such words. But Restan (99) gives the following figures: accusative frequency for clauses with normal word order, 29·9 per cent; for clauses where the object is placed before the negated predicate, 35·2 per cent; for clauses with 'marked inversion, i.e. when the object is placed in the very beginning of the clause', 40·5 per cent. The argument is clearly faulty at some stage.

If, instead of considering the general figures, a sample of the relevant clauses is looked at in detail it will be found that the case used—whether genitive or accusative—is almost invariably consistent with Morison's theory. It seems, therefore, that inversion, whether in positive or negative constructions, can serve two contradictory purposes: (*a*) as Unbegaun puts it (301), it throws the emphasis onto the direct object...

дорóгу в гóрод...указáл мне... солдáт	...a soldier showed me the road to the town...

or, as Borras and Christian put it (384), 'Just as the subject may in Russian be brought into prominence by being placed at the end of its sentence or clause, so the object may be emphasized by being placed at the beginning...

Свои угрóзы он с удовóльствием приводи́л в дéйствие... (Fedin)	His threats he took pleasure in carrying out...'

(*b*) it disposes of the direct object and leaves the reader's attention to be directed to the verb or whatever comes later in the sentence.

Despite his remark quoted above, Unbegaun says (297-8): 'The fact that the predicate comes at the beginning of the sentence does not usually throw the emphasis on to it; the shift of the predicate serves usually only to indicate the dependence of the sentence on the preceding or following elements...cf....the use of the definite article in the translation of убийцей оказался счетовод... ["the murderer turned out to be the accountant"] ("the murderer", whose identity had already been discussed).' These words read almost like a description of the situation in which an accusative would be expected by Morison's theory: the object is already known and interest is concentrated on what happens to it.

The (a) type of inversion described above would be associated with the genitive in negative constructions, because of its emphasis on the object. One example will suffice for this common construction:

— Чернов спросил:
— Свежих сводок не знаете?...
Ответа он уже не дослушал.
(Azhayev, Далеко от Москвы)

Chernov asked:
'You don't know the latest reports?'
...But he did not hear the answer out.

(The last sentence is the relevant one for the present purpose.)

The (b) type of inversion would be associated with the accusative, e.g.

...Калитин время от времени писал статьи и посылал их...в редакции...Но статьи не печатали. (Il'ina, Возвращение)

...From time to time Kalitin wrote articles and sent them to the editorial offices...But they did not print the articles.

It is obvious to the reader that it is the articles which are at issue; the point of interest, the emphasis both in general and for the purposes of negation, is on what does or does not happen to them.

...она достала из портфеля толстую книгу... а записную книжку ...не достала.
(Antonov, Избранное)

...from her briefcase she took a thick book..., but she did not take her note-book.

If the word order in the second clause were normal the parallel construction and vocabulary of the two clauses would suggest that this was a case of equal stress. However, the inversion in the second clause emphasizes the negation of the repeated verb rather than of the newly introduced object of this clause.

... возрастающие сомнения. Тревогу среди французов не могут не усиливать сообщения, подобные... (Правда, 19. XII. 64)

...growing doubts. The alarm of the French cannot but be increased by reports like...

In this case the word тревóгу is not really a new introduction but simply a re-expression of 'возрастáющие сомнéния'. The inversion serves to remind the reader of the 'alarm' from the outset and then to leave his mind free to concentrate on what is going to happen to this 'alarm' about which he already knows. (The fact that this clause contains a double negative has no special relevance. There is no reason to believe that such clauses have any essentially peculiar features.)

The conclusion to be drawn from the above remarks is that there is, despite first appearances, no contradiction between Morison's theory and Restan's statistics on accusative frequency in inversion.

B. *Verbs with the prefix недо-*

There are only four examples of these verbs in the present collection: two with accusative, two with genitive. In three cases the use is consistent with Morison's theory, e.g.

| Чижóва с дáвних пор недолюбли́-вала Антони́ну Пáвловну... (Erenburg, Óттепель) | For long enough Chizhova had not been specially fond of Antonina Pavlovna... |

Antonina Pavlovna has just been mentioned and is firmly in the reader's mind. It is Chizhova's attitude to her which is of interest.

In one case the use is not consistent with Morison:

| ...рáньше недооцéнивал э́той слóжности. (Azhayev, Далекó от Москвы́) | ...he had earlier underestimated this complexity. |

From the point of view of logic this sentence is a perfect parallel with the one quoted above: 'complication' has just been mentioned and must be in the reader's mind. An accusative would be expected.

Ward has pointed out that Ushakov's dictionary (1935–40) gives far fewer of such verbs as taking either genitive or accusative than does the Academy Dictionary (1957–61). This supports the view that usage is still changing.

C. *не directly associated with the object*

It is generally accepted that, if the negation is specifically directed to some part of the sentence other than the verb or direct object itself, then the object is in the accusative, e.g.

...име́ет не иносказа́тельное, а буква́льное значе́ние. (Пра́вда, 22. XII. 64)	...has a meaning which is not allegorical but literal.
...солда́ты не о́чень обраща́ли внима́ние на их смысл... (Kazakevich, Дом на пло́щади)	...the soldiers did not pay particular attention to their sense...

Negation of this type often leaves the sentence with a positive sense, e.g.

...предоста́вила...не то́лько свой большо́й концерт́ный зал, но и симфони́ческий орке́стр. (Пра́вда, 22. XII. 64)	...provided not only its large concert hall but a symphony orchestra as well.

However, in direct contradiction both to what might be expected in view of the above remarks and to what might be expected in view of Morison's theory, it appears that if by means of word order the negation is specifically restricted to the direct object, then again the object is in the accusative, e.g.

Я не путёвку прошу́ на куро́рт. (Azhayev, Далеко́ от Москвы́)	I'm not asking for a pass to the health resort.
Сейча́с на́до знать не се́льское хозя́йство вообще́, а знать ка́ждую культу́ру. (Пра́вда, 7. VIII. 64)	Now it is necessary to know not agriculture in general, but to know each crop.

From the learner's point of view it is convenient that the accusative is used in all of the constructions mentioned in this section, since it is not always easy to see from the word order what precisely is being negated, e.g.

...сде́лал не о́чень уда́чную попы́тку. (Leonov, Ру́сский лес)	...made a not very successful attempt.

Here it is either the adverb or the adjective plus adverb which is negated, not the noun.

This requirement for the use of the accusative outweighs any other features which might indicate the use of the genitive.

5. THE FORMULATION OF RULES

Stress must be laid on the fact that the various examples quoted above are mere illustrations, not proof. It would, for instance, be easy to produce large numbers of examples with э́то (this/that) used in the accusative; but it appears, on the basis of Restan's figures (102), that they would not constitute more than 9 per cent of a representative sample and, on the basis of the present examination, that this deviant percentage would not show any special characteristics to justify its deviation. Moreover, again on the basis of the present examination, it is probable that an appreciable number of the genitives would have this case in clear contradiction to the indications of Morison's theory. These factors point to этого itself as the determining feature and suggest that although это is used it is usually just a syntactical deviation caused by the four factors listed above (pp. 53-4). When it comes to teaching students what to do, they should be told to use этого with the exceptions indicated below in 'Summary of indications for case choice'.

It may be that, having already taken root to some extent, the use of это in the accusative will grow and that, as it grows, it will gradually conform to the pattern indicated by Morison's theory. It is, however, extraordinarily difficult to decide at what point usage with a particular feature is conforming sufficiently for the rule to be changed. If accusative usage is less than 9 per cent and these accusatives show no special recurring features to make them a recognizable group; if, in addition, the indications of Morison's theory for an accusative are frequently disregarded and a genitive is used, then it seems safe—if arbitrary—to state that the genitive is the rule, as here.

On the other hand, the use of the gerunds and participles indicates the difficulties faced in formulating a rule. Restan's sample gives accusative frequency of 12 per cent for negated gerunds and participles (100). There is no obvious characteristic of these parts of speech which could reasonably explain such a low accusative frequency in terms of Morison's theory: they would seem prima facie to be just as likely to be found in constructions leading to the accusative as to the genitive. The high genitive frequency is often explained by the fact that gerunds and participles are felt to be a literary form requiring the nineteenth-century literary norm of usage, i.e. the genitive. Yet on closer examination it is found that few examples of genitive use with negated gerunds and participles are questionable under the terms of Morison's theory, i.e. it does not appear that there is indiscriminate use of the genitive.

The explanation seems to be as follows. The gerund and participle are forms found much more frequently in narrative than in dialogue. Dialogue shows a higher accusative frequency than narrative. According to Restan (106) this 'is often only an indirect result of the use of the colloquial style, the direct reason being the structure or the form of the clauses. Thus imperative clauses are far more common in dialogue than in narrative prose (in our material 39 examples from dialogue, none from narrative prose). This is also the case in interrogative clauses (in our selection, 31 examples from dialogue, 2 from narrative prose).' It follows that the structure or form of clauses used in narrative is more likely to lead to the genitive (purely from a statistical point of view). The matter now begins to make sense, since it is easy to understand how certain structures are more likely to lead to one case or another in terms of Morison's theory. In the absence of any evidence to the contrary it would seem that clauses with gerunds or participles are simply an extreme example of the tendency of narrative to lead to a negative genitive in agreement with a Morison-type analysis.

The preceding remarks are intended to explain why features which show a fairly close similarity of accusative frequency (on Restan's figures: это, 9 per cent; gerunds and participles, 12 per cent) are not treated similarly in the present work. There is reason to prescribe этого; there is none apparent to prescribe the genitive after gerunds and participles, with the exceptions indicated in the section on sentences with equal logical stress of negation.

There is no guarantee that negative genitive/negative accusative usage is yet stabilized. Even if the present exposition proves to be correct for written Russian 1944-64 it may well have to be modified for written Russian 1964-84.

It seems unlikely that the accusative will come to be used where it at present has almost no frequency at all (e.g. with иметь, 'to have', which is highly resistant to change because of its affinity to нет, and in idioms like не производить впечатления, 'to make no impression'), since it has already had many years to make such inroads as might be possible. It is possible that accusative это will increase and conform to the indications of Morison's theory since it is a word which by its use to refer to something known often invites an accusative in that theory. It is also just possible that there may be an increase in the use with accusative of the less emphatic forms of intensive negation (i.e. ни and и rather than никакой). Restan (101) gives figures which indicate that accusative frequency with ни and и in his sample is over 4 per cent (probably much more). Occasionally such usages can almost be included in the category of equal stress, particularly if both verb and object are intensely negated. It is not, however, likely that there will be much change here since the pattern of genitive use for intensive negation is, to a large extent, in accordance with Morison's theory.

Assuming absolute awareness by all writers of the possibility of genitive/accusative distinction, there is still no reason why, in the course of time, there should not be a change of feeling about a certain function. It may, for example, be increasingly felt that indirect negation through an infinitive places the emphasis of negation on the verbs and a sort of 'accusative tyranny' could come to prevail against the indications of Morison's theory.

It is not impossible that, with the exception of certain idioms, the genitive/accusative choice could become a free one with a 50/50 distribution. This could happen because of the frequently subtle nature of the choice and the fact that, where there is a choice, it is rarely accompanied by easily recognized grammatical or lexical indicators. It seems unlikely that the accusative will in general oust the genitive since the possibility of the genitive for objects will be maintained in idioms, by animate objects and by those verbs which sometimes take a genitive object in positive statements. When used in the negative these are 'no choice' genitives and form a sufficiently large percentage of total usage to have a lasting influence.

6. SUMMARY OF INDICATIONS FOR CASE CHOICE

It is not too difficult to learn by imitation and observation how to use, for example, the dative case without understanding the usage analytically. It would, on the other hand, be extraordinarily difficult for the non-native speaker of Russian to master negative genitive/accusative usage without having some analytical understanding of the problem since there are few easily recognizable markers for case choice. Although the teaching of a foreign language as though it were a crossword or jigsaw puzzle is to some extent discredited, it may still be useful to summarize the conclusions of the present work from the point of view of the non-native speaker trying to compose a Russian sentence.

If the sentence contains any of the features listed below, the object will be in the case indicated.

Accusative

(1) хотя́ бы (i.e. where the verb is negated).

Но я не реша́лся заже́чь хотя́ бы одну́... (Paustovsky, По́весть о жи́зни)

But I couldn't decide to light even one...

(2) чуть (ли) не, ничу́ть не.

...моя́ мать вы́нуждена чи́стить карто́шку и чуть ли не полы́ мыть... (Il'ina, Возвраще́ние)

...my mother is compelled to peel potatoes and almost to wash floors...

Всё э́то ничу́ть не напомина́ло индустриа́льный пейза́ж. (Kazakevich, Дом на пло́щади)

All of this was in no way reminiscent of an industrial landscape.

(3) не счита́ть + acc. + instr. (see p. 40).

...не́мки действи́тельно не счита́ли дру́жбу с ру́сскими солда́тами национа́льным преда́тельством. (Kazakevich, Дом на пло́щади)

...the German girls really didn't regard friendship with the Russian soldiers as a betrayal of their country.

(4) едва́ (ли) не.

Ворва́вшийся ве́тер едва́ не заду́л свечу́... (Il'ina, Возвраще́ние)

The wind came rushing in and nearly blew out the candle...

(5) Various sayings and set expressions, e.g. па́лец о па́лец не уда́рить (not to raise a finger), не моро́чить го́лову (not to pull the wool over someone's eyes).

(6) не directly associated with direct object (see pp. 56–7).

Я не всё зна́ю. (Erenburg, О́ттепель)

I don't know everything.

Genitive

(1) не име́ть.

К пла́ну вку́са не име́ю. (Azhayev, Далеко́ от Москвы́)

The plan does not appeal to me. (Lit.: 'I have no taste for the plan.')

(2) Intensive negation: и, никако́й, ни (NOT како́й бы...ни).

...но не успе́л сде́лать и трёх шаго́в... (Tendryakov, Чрезвыча́йное)

...but did not manage to take even three paces...

Он не оста́вил никаки́х следо́в. (Paustovsky, По́весть о жи́зни)

He left no traces.

У него́ никогда́ не купи́ли ни одного́ этю́да. (Erenburg, О́ттепель)

Nobody has ever bought a single sketch from him.

(3) не видеть, говорить, замечать, понимать, знать (see pp. 42–4).
(4) negated verb + 'this/that' (i.e. этого) (see pp. 44–5).
(5) parts of the body (reflexive) (see pp. 45–6).
(6) unstressed zero quantity (see pp. 46–8).
(7) не бояться, хотеть, желать, etc. (direct negation only, see pp. 48–9).
Note. Accusative (6) above outweighs any genitive requirement. Accusative (3) above outweighs genitive requirements (4)–(6) inclusive.

(8) Various sayings and set expressions, e.g.

не обращать внимания	to pay no attention
не проявлять внимания	to show no interest
не давать себе отчёта	to take no account
не давать ходу, проходу, покоя, возможности	not to let move, pass, not to give peace, possibility
не придавать значения	to attach no significance
не подавать (показывать) вида/виду	to show no sign
не терять времени, памяти, надежды	not to lose time, consciousness, hope
не тратить (зря) времени	not to waste time
не внушать уважения, доверия	not to inspire respect, trust
не видеть света	(figuratively) not to see the light
не производить впечатления	to produce no impression
не принимать участия	to take no part
не играть роли	to play no part
не находить себе места	to be agitated
не сводить глаз	not to take one's eyes from
не дал бог свинье рог/рогов	God did not give pigs horns

If there are none of the above features, apply Morison's rule (see pp. 35–42).

If there are no indications for differing incidence of logical stress of negation, apply the rules for equal stress (see pp. 49–51):

(*a*) If the negated verb is gerund or participle—GENITIVE.
(*b*) If the negation is indirect through an infinitive—ACCUSATIVE.
(*c*) If the noun ends in the nominative in -a or -я—ACCUSATIVE.
(*d*) If there is a conflict between (*a*) and (*b*) or (*c*), then (*a*) prevails—GENITIVE.

(*e*) If there are none of the indications (*a*)–(*d*)—GENITIVE.

Note. It is probable that there still remains a very small group of negative constructions in which it is impossible to make a choice of case on the basis of the criteria given above because of conflicting indications. The very fact that the group is so small shows that native users of the language generally avoid these problems by expressing themselves in such a way that the conflict does not arise. The English-speaking student should follow their example.

BIBLIOGRAPHY

ALEKSEYEV, M. P. *et al.* (eds.). *Словарь русского языка* ('Academy Dictionary'). 4 vols., Государственное издательство иностранных и национальных словарей, Moscow, 1957–61.
BORRAS, F. M. & CHRISTIAN, R. F. *Russian Syntax*. Oxford University Press, 1959.
BULAKHOVSKY, L. A. *Курс русского литературного языка* (5th ed.). Радянська Школа, Kiev, 1952.
BUTORIN, D. I. *Винительный и родительный падежи прямого объекта в русском литературном языке XIX–XX веков*. Ленинградский государственный педагогический институт, Leningrad, 1953.
DOBROMYSLOV, V. A. & ROZENTAL', D. E. *Трудные вопросы грамматики и правописания*. Учпедгиз, Moscow, 1955.
FINKEL', A. M. & BAZHENOV, N. M. *Современный русский литературный язык* (2nd ed.). Радянська Школа, Kiev, 1954.
FLECKENSTEIN, C. 'Zur Frage des Kasusgebrauchs nach verneinten Transitiva im Russischen', *Wissenschaftliche Zeitschrift der Martin-Luther-Universität Halle–Wittenberg*. 1961, X/1, 213–20.
GVOZDYOV, A. N. *Современный русский литературный язык*. Учпедгиз, Moscow, 1958.
JAKOBSON, R. 'Beitrag zur allgemeinen Kasuslehre.' (Etudes dédiées au quatrième congrès de linguistes.) *Travaux du cercle linguistique de Prague*. Prague, 1936, No. 6, 240–88.
KOUT, I. 'Прямое дополнение в отрицательных предложениях в русском языке', *Русский язык в школе*. Просвещение, Moscow, 1960, No. 2, 27–32.
LÉPISSIER, J. 'Du génitif-accusatif inanimé en vieux slave', *Revue des études slaves*. Paris, 1964, XL, 126–37.
MAGNER, T. F. 'Negation and case selection in Russian', *Word*. New York, 1955, II, 531–41.
MARYNIAK, I. 'Dopełnienie bliższe przy czasownikach zaprzeczonych we współczesnym rosyjskim języku literackim', *Slavia Orientalis*. Warsaw, 1959, Rocznik VIII, Nr. 4, 111–19.
MORISON, W. A. *Studies in Russian Forms and Uses—the present gerund and active participle*. Faber, London, 1959.
MORISON, W. A. 'Logical stress and grammatical form in Russian', *Slavonic and East European Review*. London, 1964, XLII, No. 99, 292–7.
PANINA, A. F. 'Родительный и винительный падежи при глаголах с

отрицанием в русском литературном языке конца XVIII–начала XIX в.', *Дослідження з української та російської мов*. Радянська Школа, Kiev, 1964, pp. 197–211.

PESHKOVSKY, A. M. *Русский синтаксис в научном освещении* (7th ed.). Учпедгиз, Moscow, 1956.

RESTAN, P. A. 'The objective case in negative clauses in Russian', *Scando-Slavica*. Copenhagen, 1960, VI, 92–112.

RESTAN, P. A. 'Konkurransen mellom nektet genitiv og nektet akkusativ i moderne russisk (1918–1959).' M.A. dissertation, University of Oslo, 1959. (Unpublished except in the summary in *Scando-Slavica*.)

ROZENTAL', D. E. *Modern Russian Usage*. Pergamon, London, 1963.

SAFAREWICZOWA, H. 'Forma dopełnienia bliższego w rosyjskim zdaniu zaprzeczonym. Część I', *Slavia Orientalis*. Warsaw, 1959, Rocznik VIII, Nr. 4, 77–109. 'Część II', *ibid*. Warsaw, 1960, Rocznik IX, Nr. 1, 69–137.

SHAKHMATOV, A. A. *Синтаксис русского языка* (reprint of 2nd ed.). Mouton, The Hague, 1963.

THOMSON, A. 'Beiträge zur Kasuslehre. III. Zur Genetivrektion des Verbums im Baltischslavischen', *Indogermanische Forschungen*. Strassburg, 1911/12, XXIX, 249–59.

UGLITSKY, Z. 'Accusative and genitive with transitive verbs preceded by a negative in contemporary Russian', *Slavonic and East European Review*. London, 1955–6, XXXIV, 377–87.

UNBEGAUN, B. O. *Russian Grammar*. Oxford University Press, 1957.

USHAKOV, D. N. *et al*. Толковый словарь русского языка. 4 vols., Огиз, Moscow, 1935–40.

VINOGRADOV, V. V., ISTRINA, YE. S. & BARKHUDAROV, S. G. (eds.). *Грамматика русского языка*. 3 vols., Академия Наук, Moscow, 1952–4.

WARD, D. *The Russian Language Today*. Hutchinson, London, 1965.